Frommer's®

MEMORABLE WALKS IN NEW YORK

3rd Edition

by
Reid Bramblett

MACMILLAN • USA

ABOUT THE AUTHOR

A resident of Brooklyn's Park Slope neighborhood, **Reid Bramblett** is an alumnus of Macmillan Travel's editorial office, and is the author of *Frommer's Tuscany and Umbria* and *The Complete Idiot's Guide to Europe.*

MACMILLAN TRAVEL

A Simon & Schuster Macmillan Company
1633 Broadway
New York, NY 10019

Find us online at **www.frommers.com**

Copyright © 1998 by Simon & Schuster, Inc.
Maps copyright © by Simon & Schuster, Inc.

MACMILLAN is a registered trademark of Macmillan, Inc. FROMMER'S is a registered trademark of Arthur Frommer. Used under license.

ISBN 0-02862133-6
ISSN 1081-339x

Editor: Vanessa Rosen
Production Editor: Mark Enochs
Map Editor: Douglas Stallings
Design by designLab
Digital Cartography by Ortelius Design

SPECIAL SALES

Bulk purchases (10+ copies) of Frommer's and selected Macmillan travel guides are available to corporations, organizations, mail-order catalogs, institutions, and charities at special discounts. For more information write to Special Sales, Macmillan General Reference, 1633 Broadway, New York, NY 10019.

Manufactured in the United States of America

Contents

Introducing New York   1

The Walking Tours

1 Lower Manhattan/The Financial District   8
2 Chinatown   22
3 The Jewish Lower East Side   37
4 SoHo   48
5 Greenwich Village Literary Tour   67
6 The East Village   92
7 Midtown   114
8 Central Park   128
9 The Upper West Side   140
10 The Upper East Side   153

Index   165

LIST OF MAPS

The Tours at a Glance   3

The Walking Tours

Lower Manhattan/The Financial District   10
Chinatown   23
The Jewish Lower East Side   39
SoHo   51
Greenwich Village Literary Tour   68–69
The East Village   94
Midtown   115
Central Park   130–131
The Upper West Side   142
The Upper East Side   155

• • • • • • •

Acknowledgements

Reid wishes to thank Vanessa Rosen and Lisa Renaud for the fine editorial job, and Frances Sayers, who helped walk some of the tours and braved the mysterious ingesting of unknown objects in the dim sum restaurants of Chinatown. Thanks also go out to Frank Bramblett, Margo Margolis, and Marina Adams—a trio of painters who helped make sense of New York's gallery scene.

Find Frommer's Online

Arthur Frommer's Outspoken Encyclopedia of Travel (www.frommers.com) offers more than 6,000 pages of up-to-the-minute travel information—including the latest bargains and candid, personal articles updated daily by Arthur Frommer himself. No other Web site offers such comprehensive and timely coverage of the world of travel.

An Invitation to the Reader

In researching this book, I discovered many wonderful sights, restaurants, and more. I'm sure you'll discover more. Please tell me about them, so I can share the information with your fellow travelers in upcoming editions. If you were disappointed with a recommendation, I want to know that, too. Please write to:

Reid Bramblett
℅ *Frommer's Memorable Walks in New York*
Macmillan Travel
1633 Broadway
New York, NY 10019

An Additional Note

Please be advised that travel information is subject to change at any time. The author, editors, and publisher cannot be held responsible for the experiences of readers while traveling. Your safety is important to us, however, so we encourage you to stay alert and be aware of your surroundings. Keep a close eye on cameras, purses, and wallets, all favorite targets of thieves and pickpockets.

Introducing
New York

It's next to impossible to get a handle on the big picture of New York all at once. The best way to get to know this amazingly complex city is to do as New Yorkers do—concentrate on small nooks and crannies rather than the whole. Define the city through its neighborhoods and pay close attention to every detail of architecture, image, and life.

As you explore, you'll see tiny, funky flower gardens that have sprung up around sidewalk trees. Or, you might come across a shop that sells just lightbulbs. In other parts, the rocks in Central Park acquire names; a museum of Ukrainian heritage opens; and Zabar's searches for a new unknown cheese from the Pyrenees to introduce to Upper West Siders.

That's why walking tours are truly the only way to see this city. To get anywhere near understanding New York, you need to grab just one chunk of it at a time, turn it over carefully in your mind, examine its history, and figure out what makes it tick. A large-scale New York may seem like an enormous, chaotic, dirty, expensive, frightening metropolis. But on the small scale, in the details, New York gives up its secrets. It started as a conglomeration of small communities and from these roots, it has grown into one of the most fascinating and vibrant cities on earth.

1

MIXED NUTS & MICHELANGELOS

A sizable cast of regular characters inhabits the city's streets. Strolling about, you might encounter the Tree Man, who is always festooned with leafy branches; the portly fellow with a long white beard who dresses as Santa Claus all year long (he's Jewish, no less); or the man who pushes a baby carriage with a large white duck inside.

Quentin Crisp once said, "Everyone in Manhattan is a star or a star manqué, and every flat surface in the island is a stage." Street performers run the gamut from a tuxedoed gent who does Fred-and-Ginger ballroom dances with a life-size rag doll (usually in front of the Metropolitan Museum) to the circus-caliber acrobats and stand-up comics who attract large audiences in Washington Square Park. There are mimes and musicians—everything from steel drum bands and Ecuadorian flute players to the pianist with his candelabra-adorned baby grand perched atop a truck.

Street artists abound. Here and there, especially in the East Village, little mosaic-tile designs pop up to adorn the sidewalk and streetlight pedestals. An area artist created them from cracked plates and crockery picked up from people's trash. In the 1980s, street painting became especially popular. Some sketched purple footsteps and stenciled animal and fish designs on sidewalks, others drew attention to the crime rate by painting body outlines all over the place. But in New York, nothing can remain small-time for long; the graffiti became an established art form, and the more highbrow street doodlers like Keith Haring and Kenny Schraf became international stars.

TWIN TOWERS, TENEMENTS & TOWN HOUSES

New York is a city of extraordinarily diverse architecture. The Financial District's neoclassic "temples"—embellished with allegorical statuary, massive colonnades, vaulted domes, and vast marble lobbies—stand side by side with the soaring skyscrapers that make up the world's most famous skyline. Across the bridge are the tranquil tree-shaded streets of Brooklyn Heights—a charming enclave of brownstones, churches, and landmark buildings, with a riverside promenade offering scenic views of the Manhattan skyline and the Statue of Liberty.

The history of immigrant groups is manifest in the ramshackle tenements of Chinatown and the Lower East Side. SoHo's

The Tours at a Glance

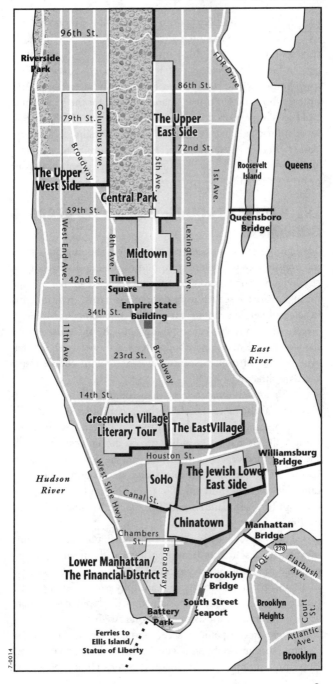

cast-iron facades hearken back to the ideals of the industrial era, when design first encountered the principles of mass production, and became accessible to everyone.

In Greenwich Village, you'll see the stately Greek Revival town houses, where Henry James and Edith Wharton lived. And uptown, magnificent private mansions built for the Vanderbilts and the Whitneys overlook Central Park, itself one of the world's most impressive urban greenbelts. No wonder quintessential New Yorker Woody Allen was inspired to pay tribute to the city's architectural diversity by including an otherwise gratuitous tour of his favorite buildings in *Hannah and Her Sisters.*

THE NEIGHBORHOODS: BOK CHOY, BEADS & BOHEMIANS

Though their city has been called more of a boiling pot than a melting pot, New Yorkers are proud of the ethnic diversity of city neighborhoods. From the days of the early Dutch settlers, immigrants have striven to re-create their native environments in selected neighborhoods. Hence, the restaurants of Mulberry Street, with convivial cafes spilling onto the sidewalks, evoke the streets of Palermo. Orthodox Jews still operate shops that evolved from turn-of-the-century pushcarts along cobblestoned Orchard Street.

Chinatown, home to more than 160,000 Chinese, is probably New York's most extensive ethnic area, and it's continually expanding, gobbling up parts of the old Lower East Side and Little Italy. Its narrow, winding streets are lined with noodle shops, Chinese vegetable vendors, small curio stores, Buddhist temples, Chinese movie theaters, and several hundred restaurants. New Yorkers don't talk about going out for Chinese food—they opt for Szechuan, Hunan, Cantonese, Mandarin, Fukien, or dim sum.

The East Village has a sizable Ukrainian population, whose inexpensive restaurants (featuring borscht, blini, and pierogi) enhance the local culinary scene. Ukrainian folk arts, such as intricately painted Easter eggs, beautifully embroidered peasant blouses, and illuminated manuscripts, are displayed in local shops and even warrant a museum on Second Avenue.

There are Hispanic, Czech, German, Greek, Hungarian, Indian, Russian, Arab, and West Indian parts of town as well. But ethnic groups are not the only factor defining New York neighborhoods. On the streets around Broadway from Macy's to about 39th Street you're in the heart of the Garment District, where artists race through the streets carrying large portfolios of next season's designs, trying not to collide with workers pushing racks of this year's fashions. Also distinct are the city's bead, book, feather, fur, flower, toy, diamond, and, of course, theater districts.

Different neighborhoods also attract diverse residents. The Upper East Side is where old money lives; rumpled intellectuals prefer the Upper West Side. Young trendies and aging hippies live in the East Village, old bohemians in the West Village. The West Village and Chelsea are home to sizable gay populations, and artists and the yuppies who emulate them hang out in SoHo. These are largely generalizations, of course, but each area does have a distinct flavor. You probably won't find designer clothing on St. Marks Place. On the other hand, a Madison Avenue boutique is unlikely to carry S&M leather wear. Midtown is the city's main shopping area, site of our ever-diminishing grand department stores. And Broadway dissects the town diagonally; though it's most famous for the glitz and glitter of the Great White Way, it actually spans Manhattan from Battery Park to the Bronx.

IF YOU CAN MAKE IT HERE . . .

The song has become a cliché, but like many clichés it's true. New York is, and always has been, a mecca for the ambitious. And though only a small percentage of the ardently aspiring become famous—or even manage to eke out a living—the effort keeps New Yorkers keen-witted, intense, on the cutting edge.

New York is America's business and financial center, where major deals have gone down over power lunches since the days when Thomas Jefferson and Alexander Hamilton chose the site for the nation's capital over a meal at a Manhattan restaurant. Every major book and magazine publisher is based here. It's an international media and fashion center as well. New York galleries set worldwide art trends. And a lead in a play in Galveston, Texas, is less impressive than a bit part on Broadway. (At least New Yorkers think so.)

For that reason, almost every famous artist, writer, musician, and actor has, at one time or another, resided in Gotham.

The waitress serving you in a coffee shop may be tomorrow's Glenn Close; your cab driver may make the cover of *Time*. And since they're all over town, you'll probably even rub elbows with an already-acclaimed celebrity or two as well. If not, there's always the thrill of downing a drink or two in bars that Dylan Thomas or Jackson Pollock frequented, visiting the Greenwich Village haunts of the Beat Generation, peering up at what was once Edgar Allan Poe's bedroom window, or dining at the Algonquin Hotel where Round Table wits Dorothy Parker, Alexander Woollcott, and George S. Kaufman traded barbs in the 1920s.

The presence of so many movers and shakers gives New York vitality and sophistication. When you study film at the New School your lecturers are Martin Scorsese, Sydney Pollack, Barry Levinson, and Neil Simon. Pavarotti's at one Met, everyone from Raphael to Rembrandt is at the other. Few bookstores are as great as the Strand, no food shop as alluring as Zabar's (except perhaps Balducci's or Dean and Deluca), no department store a match for Bloomie's and Macy's, no mall comparable to Orchard Street. Where else can you easily satisfy a craving for Thai noodles at 3am? Or have your choice of dozens of art-house movies nightly, many of which will never play in most American towns?

Visitors often question how New Yorkers stand the constant noise, the rudeness, the filth, the outrageous rents and prices, the crime, the crazies, or even one another. But though New Yorkers frequently talk about leaving the city, few ever do. They've created a unique frame of reference, and it doesn't travel well. The constant stimulation feeds Gothamites' creativity. To quote theatrical impresario Joseph Papp, "Creative people get inspiration from their immediate environment, and New York has the most immediate environment in the world."

ORIENTATION

Main Arteries & Streets Laid out on a grid system (except for the village), Manhattan is the easiest of the boroughs to negotiate. Avenues run north (uptown) and south (downtown), while the streets run east to west (crosstown). Broadway runs south to north diagonally across the grid.

Both avenues and streets are numbered consecutively; streets from south to north (1st Street is downtown just above Houston Street); and avenues from east to west, (with 5th Avenue in the center) from First Avenue near the East River to Twelfth Avenue near the Hudson River. The only exceptions are the three named avenues on the East Side: Madison (east of Fifth Avenue), Park (which would be Fourth Avenue), and Lexington (west of third Avenue). Sixth Avenue is also called the Avenue of the Americas.

Fifth Avenue is the dividing line between the East Side and West Side, so an address on West 43rd Street will be west of Fifth Avenue. All east-west street addresses are counted from Fifth Avenue, starting at no. 1 on either side of Fifth and increasing in number as they move away from Fifth Avenue. In other words, at the corner of Fifth Avenue and 35th Street, to the east you'll find 1 East 35th St., and to the west will be 1 West 35th St.

A few avenues acquire new names as they move uptown: Eighth Avenue becomes Central Park West above 59th Street, Ninth Avenue becomes Columbus Avenue above 69th Street, and Tenth Avenue becomes Amsterdam above 72nd Street. Beware: Unlike other cities, addresses on avenues don't move up a steady number each block.

The handy grid pattern wasn't imposed on the older downtown sections below 14th Street on the West Side, or below Houston Street on the East Side. Downtown streets have names rather than numbers, and in the oldest sections, roads follow the old street plans of the various small villages that long ago joined together to become

Lower
Manhattan/
The Financial
District

Start: Battery Park/U.S. Customs House.

Subway: Take the 5 to Bowling Green, the 1 or 9 to South Ferry, or the N or R to Whitehall Street.

Finish: The Municipal Building.

Time: Approximately 3 hours.

Best Time: Any weekday, when the wheels of finance are spinning and lower Manhattan is a maelstrom of frantic activity.

Worst Time: Weekends, when most buildings and all the financial markets are closed.

The narrow winding streets of the Financial District occupy the earliest-settled area of Manhattan, where the Dutch established the colony of Nieuw Amsterdam in the early 17th century. Before their arrival, downtown was part of a vast forest, a lush hunting ground for the Native Americans, inhabited by mountain lions, bobcats, beavers, white-tailed deer, and wild turkeys. A hunting path, which later evolved into Broadway, extended from the Battery to the present City Hall Park.

Today this section of the city, much like Nieuw Amsterdam, centers on commerce. Wall Street is America's most cogent symbol of money and power; bulls and bears have replaced the wild beasts of the forest, and conservatively attired lawyers, stockbrokers, bankers, and businesspeople have supplanted the Native Americans and Dutchmen who once traded otter skins and beaver pelts on these very streets.

A highlight of this tour is the Financial District's architecture, in which the neighborhood's modern manifestations and grand historical structures are dramatically juxtaposed: Colonial, 18th-century Georgian/Federal, and 19th-century neoclassical buildings stand in the shadow of colossal skyscrapers.

• • • • • • • • • • • • • • • •

The subways all exit in or near **Battery Park,** an expanse of green at Manhattan's tip resting entirely upon landfill—an old strategy of the Dutch to expand their settlement farther into the bay. The original tip of Manhattan ran somewhere right along Battery Place, which borders the north side of the park. State Street flanks the park's east side, and stretched along it, filling the space below Bowling Green, squats the Beaux Arts bulk of the old:

1. **U.S. Customs House,** since 1994, home to the Smithsonian's National Museum of the American Indian (☎ **212/668-6624**). The giant statues lining the front of this granite 1907 structure personify *Asia* (pondering philosophically), *America* (bright-eyed and bushy-tailed), *Europe* (decadent, whose time has passed), *and Africa* (sleeping), and were carved by Daniel Chester French of Lincoln Memorial fame. The most interesting, if unintentional, sculptural statement—keeping in mind the building's new

Lower Manhattan/The Financial District

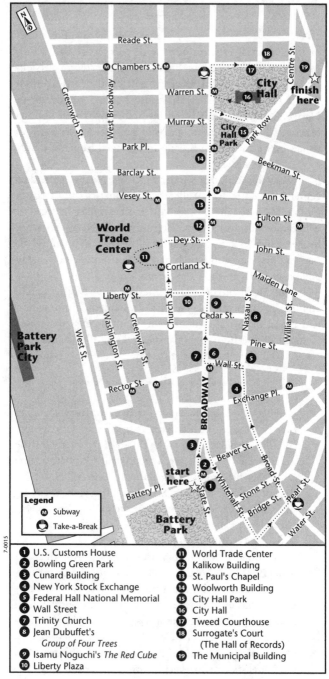

Legend
- Ⓜ Subway
- 🥤 Take-a-Break

1. U.S. Customs House
2. Bowling Green Park
3. Cunard Building
4. New York Stock Exchange
5. Federal Hall National Memorial
6. Wall Street
7. Trinity Church
8. Jean Dubuffet's
   Group of Four Trees
9. Isamu Noguchi's *The Red Cube*
10. Liberty Plaza
11. World Trade Center
12. Kalikow Building
13. St. Paul's Chapel
14. Woolworth Building
15. City Hall Park
16. City Hall
17. Tweed Courthouse
18. Surrogate's Court
    (The Hall of Records)
19. The Municipal Building

purpose—is the giant seated woman to the left of the entrance representing America. The young, upstart America is surrounded by references to Native America: Mayan pictographs adorning her throne, Quetzalcoatl under her foot, a shock of corn in her lap, and the generic plains Indian scouting out from over her shoulder. Look behind her throne for the stylized crow figure—an important animal in many native cultures, usually playing a trickster character in myths, which is probably why he's hiding back here.

The airy oval rotunda inside was frescoed by Reginald Marsh to glorify the shipping industry (and, by extension, the customs office once here). The free museum, open daily 10am to 5pm, hosts a roster of well-curated exhibits highlighting Native cultures, history, and contemporary issues in sophisticated and thought-provoking ways.

As you exit the building, directly in front of you sits the pretty little oasis of:

2. **Bowling Green Park.** This is probably the spot, or at least near enough, where in 1626 Dutchman Peter Minuit gave glass beads and other trinkets worth about 60 Guilders ($24) to a group of Indians, and then claimed he had thereby bought Manhattan. Now the local Indians didn't consider that they owned this island—not because they didn't believe in property (that's a colonial myth), as they did have their own territories nearby. But Manhattan (which in local language means "hilly island") was considered communal hunting ground, shared by several different groups. So it isn't clear what the Indians thought the trinkets meant. Either (a) they just thought the exchange was a formal way, one to which they were accustomed, of closing an agreement to extend the shared hunting use of the island to this funny-looking group of pale people with yellow beards, or (b) they were knowingly selling land that they didn't own in the first place, thus performing the first shrewd real-estate deal of the Financial District. They probably then told Minuit they also had this bridge to sell, just up the river a ways, but he was too busy fortifying his little town of Nieuw Amsterdam to listen.

Although today just another lunch spot for stockbrokers, when King George III repealed the hated Stamp Act in 1770, New Yorkers magnanimously raised a statue of him here. The statue lasted 5 years, until the day the Declaration of Independence was read to the public in front of City Hall (now Federal Hall) and a crowd rushed down Broadway to topple the statue, chop it up, melt it down, and transform it into 42,000 bullets, which they later used to shoot the British.

The park also marks the start of Broadway. Walk up the left side of Broadway; at no. 25 is the:

3. **Cunard Building,** now a post office but in 1921 the ticketing room for Cunard, one of the world's most glamorous shipping and cruise lines and proprietors of the *QEII*. Cunard established the first passenger steamship between Europe and the Americas, and in this still-impressive Great Hall, you once could book passage on any one of their famous fantastically unfortunate ships, from the *Lusitania* (blown up by the Germans) to the *Titanic*. The poorly lit and deteriorating churchlike ceiling inside is covered with Ezra Winter paintings of the ships of Columbus, Sir Francis Drake, and Leif Eriksson, among others.

As you exit the building, cross to the traffic island to pat the enormous bronze **bull,** symbol of a strong stock market, ready to charge up Broadway. This instant icon began as a practical joke by Italian sculptor Arturo DiModica, who originally stuck it in front of the New York Stock Exchange building in the middle of the night. The unamused brokers had it promptly removed, and it eventually got placed here.

Take a Break Fraunces Tavern, 54 Pearl St. (☎ 212/269-0144), is listed as a place to eat, but it's also a legitimate stop on the tour. To reach Fraunces Tavern, head south again, around the left side of the U.S. Customs House on Whitehall Street. Take a left onto Pearl Street; just past Broad Street stretches a historic block lined with (partially rebuilt) 18th- and 19th-century buildings.

The two upper stories house the Fraunces Tavern Museum, where you can view the room in which Washington's historic farewell took place (today set up to represent a typical 18th-century tavern room) and see other American history exhibits. A small admission is charged. Hours are Monday through Friday from 10am to 4:45pm and Saturdays from noon to 4pm.

The main floor contains a posh, oak-paneled dining room with a working fireplace. Tables are set with pewter plates. The menu features steaks, seafood, pasta dishes, and colonial fare such as Yankee pot roast. A good buy here is the three-course fixed-price lunch for $17.76. Or you can opt for pub fare in the more moderately priced Tap Room, which has plush burgundy leather furnishings and walls hung with hunting trophies. Reservations are suggested at both. The restaurant is open weekdays for breakfast 7 to 10am and for lunch 11:30am to 4pm; the Tap Room is open daily from 11:30am.

From Fraunces Tavern, head straight up Broad Street. At no. 20, on the left, is the visitor's entrance to the:

4. **New York Stock Exchange** (☎ 212/656-5168), which came into being in 1792, when merchants met daily under a nearby buttonwood tree to try and pass off to each other the U.S. bonds that had been sold to fund the Revolutionary War. By 1903, they were trading stocks of publicly held companies in this Corinthian-columned beaux arts "temple" designed by George Post. Close to 2,500 companies are listed on the exchange, trading 79 billion shares valued around $4.5 trillion.

Inside you can learn all about stock trading, view exhibits and a short film on the history and workings of the stock market, and watch the frenzied action on the trading floor—color-coded capitalists oversee the changing of hands of more than 200 million stocks daily. The observation platform has been glassed in since the 1960s when Abbie Hoffman and Jerry Rubin created chaos by tossing dollar bills onto the exchange floor. Admission for this self-guided tour is free, open weekdays between 9:15am and 4pm (last entry at 3:15pm). Tickets, each for a set time later in the day (if you arrive early, you may be able just to go in), are handed out on a first-come first-served basis.

After the New York Stock Exchange, continue north (left) up Broad St. At the end of the block you'll see the Parthenon-inspired:

5. **Federal Hall National Memorial,** 26 Wall St. at Nassau Street (☎ 212/264-8700). Fronted by 32-foot fluted marble Doric columns, this imposing 1842 neoclassical temple is

most famous for the history of the old British City Hall building, later called Federal Hall, that once stood here. Peter Zenger, publisher of the outspoken *Weekly Journal,* stood trial in 1735 for "seditious libel" against Royal Gov. William Cosby. Defended brilliantly by Alexander Hamilton, Zenger's eventual acquittal (based on the grounds that anything you printed that was true, even if it wasn't very nice, couldn't be construed as libel) set the precedent for freedom of the press, later guaranteed in the Bill of Rights, which was drafted and signed inside this building.

New York's first major rebellion against British authority occurred here when the Stamp Act Congress met in 1765 to protest King George III's policy of "taxation without representation." J.Q.A. Ward's 1883 statue of George Washington on the steps commemorates the spot of the first presidential inauguration, in 1789. Congress met here after the revolution, when New York was briefly the nation's capital.

Exhibits within (open Monday to Friday 9am to 5pm) elucidate these events along with other aspects of American history. Admission is free.

Facing Federal Hall, turn left up the road that has become the symbol of high finance the world over:

6. **Wall Street.** It is narrow, just a few short blocks long, and started out as a service road that ran along the fortified wall the Dutch erected in 1653 to defend against Indian attack. (Gov. Petyer Stuyvesant's settlers had at first played off tribes against each other in order to trick them into more and more land cessation, but the native groups quickly realized their real enemies were the Dutch.)

Wall St. hits Broadway across the street from:

7. **Trinity Church** (☎ 212/602-0800). Serving God and Mammon, this Wall Street house of worship—with neo-Gothic flying buttresses, beautiful stained-glass windows, and vaulted ceilings—was designed by Richard Upjohn and consecrated in 1846. At that time its 280-foot spire dominated the skyline. Its main doors, embellished with biblical scenes, were inspired in part by Ghiberti's famed doors on Florence's Baptistery.

The first church on this site went up in 1697 and burned down in 1776. The church runs a brief tour weekdays at

2pm. There's a small museum at the end of the left aisle displaying documents (including the 1697 church charter from King William III), photographs, replicas of the Hamilton-Burr duel pistols, and other items. Capt. James Lawrence, whose famous last words were "Don't give up the ship," and Alexander Hamilton (against the south fence, next to steamboat inventor Robert Fulton) are buried in the churchyard, where the oldest grave dates from 1681.

Thursdays at 1pm, Trinity holds its Noonday Concert series of chamber music and orchestral concerts. Call ☎ 212/602-0747 for details.

Take a left out of the church and walk two short blocks up Broadway. As you pass Cedar Street, look (don't walk) to your right, across Broadway, and down Cedar and you'll see, at the end of the street:

8. **Jean Dubuffet's *Group of Four Trees,*** installed in 1972 in the artist's patented style: amorphous mushroomlike white shapes traced with undulating black lines. Dubuffet considered these drawings in three dimensions "which extend and expand into space."

Closer at hand, in front of the tall black Marine Midlank Bank building on Broadway between Cedar and Libery streets, is:

9. **Isamu Noguchi's 1967 *The Red Cube,*** another famed outdoor sculpture of downtown Manhattan. Noguchi fancied that this rhomboid "cube"—balancing on its corner and shot through with a cylinder of empty space—represented chance, like the "rolling of the dice." It is appropriately located in the gilt-edged gambling den that is the financial district.

As you're looking at the Cube across Broadway, behind you is the tiny square called:

10. **Liberty Plaza,** a block off Liberty street with some benches and shade for lunching CEOs. Turn left and walk through the park, heading east toward Trinity Place. Mingling among the flesh-and-blood office workers seated here is one in bronze, called *Double Check* (1982), by realist American sculptor J. Seward Johnson Jr.

At Trinity Place, take a right. A short block up on the left will open the grand plaza of the:

11. **World Trade Center (WTC),** bounded by Vesey, West, Liberty, and Church streets and best known for its famous 110-story twin towers. Still intact despite a terrorist bombing in early 1993, the WTC (opened in 1970 under the auspices of the Port Authority) is an immense complex. Its 12 million square feet of rentable office space house more than 350 firms and organizations. About 50,000 people work in its precincts, and some 70,000 others (tourists and businesspeople) visit them each day. The complex occupies 16 acres and includes, in addition to the towers, the sleek 22-story Marriott Hotel, a plaza the size of four football fields, an underground shopping mall, and several restaurants, most notably the spectacular Windows on the World.

The plaza, like much of downtown, is rich in outdoor sculpture, including the polished black granite miniature mountains as you enter crafted by Japanese artist Masayuki Nagare(1972). Fritz Keonig's 25-foot-high bronze morphing sphere (1971) forms the centerpiece of the plaza's wide fountain. Hang a right here between two of the squat black glass buildings to get a glance of Alexander Calder's *Three Wings.* Take particular notice of the curving, metal, winglike flanges, riveted together and painted red.

Do an about-face to return to the central plaza. The left-hand of the twin towers is 2 World Trade Center. As you enter on the mezzanine level, to your left, you'll see a 1974 tapestry by Spanish artist Joan Miró and a TKTS booth if you want to pick up half-price tickets to one of tonight's Broadway or off-Broadway shows. The real thing to do, of course, is head around the elevator banks to the right to buy tickets and whiz up to the 107th-floor Observation Deck, where you are treated to a 1,377-foot perspective of the city and New York Harbor. From there, be sure to ascend to the 110th-floor rooftop promenade, the world's highest open-air viewing platform, for even more magnificent views. Observation Deck facilities are open daily from 9:30am to 9:30pm (until 11pm June to September).

☕ **Take a Break**   To enjoy those 107th-floor views to the fullest, consider dining "a quarter mile high in the sky" at **Windows on the World,** One World Trade Center (☎ **212/524-7000** for information, 212/524-7011 for reservations). The 1993 World Trade Center bombing spurred a $25 million renovation of the famed dining spot. Now 130,680 square feet of curving lines and undulating floors make up three restaurants with menus as memorable as the views. The most accessible restaurant during lunch is the "Greatest Bar on Earth," a casually conservative spot (no jeans or sneakers) with airy spaces, a trio of bars serving everything from wine to sushi, and a sweeping view of the East River. It's open for lunch Monday to Friday noon to 2pm, with bar and food service also from 4pm to 1am. There are also a handful of seats in the main restaurant open to nonmembers (try to reserve ahead; jacket required), featuring the sumptuous spread of a $40 lunch buffet and a view of Manhattan. The restaurant is open Monday to Friday noon to 2pm, Sunday for brunch 11am to 2:30pm. For a quick meal, there's a Sbarro's snack bar on the **107th-floor observation deck of WTC2.** In summer, you might want to bring your own lunch as there are outdoor cafes with tables under trees and umbrellas on the plaza.

Alternatively, you might want to explore the varied dining choices—everything from pub fare to gourmet pizzas—offered under the enormous, 120-foot-high glass-and-steel atrium of the Winter Garden (featuring 45-foot palms from the Mojave Desert) in the **World Financial Center.** The atrium overlooks a yacht harbor and a pleasant cement park, with outdoor tables available weather permitting. The World Financial Center is behind the WTC complex. As you exit WTC 2 (the twin tower with the observation deck), walk straight, keeping the front side of WTC 1 (the other twin tower) on your left, then turn left at its corner. To your right, tucked between the back corners of WTC 1 and the squat black office building next door, are a set of doors. These open onto a long, glassed-in corridor running off to your left, suspended over the highway, that leads into the Financial Center's atrium.

Walk out the front side of WTC plaza again the way you came in, cross Church street, and head straight down Dey Street, which is in front of you, back to Broadway. Take a left, and on your left is the:

12. **Kalikow Building,** at 195 Broadway. This 1915–22 neoclassic tower, formerly AT&T headquarters, has more exterior columns than any other building in the world. The

25-story structure rests on a Doric colonnade, with Ionic colonnades above. The lobby evokes a Greek temple with a forest of massive fluted columns. The building's tower crown is modeled on the Mausoleum of Halicarnassus, the great Greek monument of antiquity. The bronze panels over the entranceway by Paul Manship (sculptor of Rockefeller Center's Prometheus) symbolize wind, air, fire, and earth.

Continue south on Broadway. The next block contains the small:

13. **St. Paul's Chapel,** between Vesey and Fulton streets, New York's only surviving prerevolutionary church. Under the east portico is a 1789 monument to Gen. Richard Montgomery, one of the first revolutionary patriots to die in battle. During the 2 years that New York was the nation's capital, George Washington worshipped at this Georgian chapel belonging to Trinity Church and dating from 1764; his "pew" is on the right side of the church. Built by Thomas McBean, with a templelike portico and fluted Ionic columns supporting a massive pediment, the chapel resembles London's St. Martin's-in-the-Fields. Explore the small graveyard where 18th- and early 19th-century notables rest in peace and modern businesspeople sit for lunch. Trinity's Noonday Concert series is held here on Mondays.

Continue up Broadway, crossing Vesey and Barclay Streets, and at 233 Broadway is the:

14. **Woolworth Building.** This soaring "Cathedral of Commerce" cost Frank W. Woolworth $13.5 million worth of nickels and dimes in 1913. Designed by Cass Gilbert, it was the world's tallest edifice until 1930, when surpassed by the Chrysler Building. At its opening, Pres. Woodrow Wilson pressed a button from the White House that illuminated the building's 80,000 electric lightbulbs. The neo-Gothic architecture is rife with spires, gargoyles, flying buttresses, vaulted ceilings, 16th-century–style stone-as-lace traceries, castlelike turrets, and a churchlike interior.

Step into the lofty marble entrance arcade to view the gleaming mosaic, Byzantine-style ceiling and gold-leafed, neo-Gothic cornices. The corbels (carved figures under the crossbeams) in the lobby include whimsical portraits of the building's engineer Gunwald Aus measuring a girder (above the staircase to the left of the main door), Gilbert holding a miniature model of the building, and Woolworth counting coins (both above the left-hand corridor of elevators). Stand near the security guard's central podium and crane your neck for a glimpse at Paul Jennewein's murals of *Commerce* and *Labor,* half hidden up on the mezzanine.

"A growing city built on a narrow peninsula is unable to expand laterally, and must, therefore, soar. The problem was how to make it soar with dignity, and the problem has been solved . . ."
—From a 1921 article in *The Times* of London praising the Woolworth Building

---

To get an overview of the Woolworth's architecture, cross Broadway. On this side of the street, you'll find scurrying city officials and greenery that together make up:

15. **City Hall Park,** a 250-year-old green surrounded by landmark buildings. A Frederick MacMonnies statue near the southwest corner of the park depicts Nathan Hale at age 21, having just uttered his famous words before execution: "I only regret that I have but one life to lose for my country." Northeast of City Hall in the park is a statue of Horace Greeley (seated with newspaper in hand) by J.Q.A. Ward. This small park has been a burial ground for paupers and the site of public executions, parades, and protests.

It is the setting for:

16. **City Hall,** the seat of municipal government, housing the offices of the mayor and his staff, the city council, and other city agencies. City Hall combines Georgian and French Renaissance styles, designed by Joseph F. Mangin and John McComb Jr. in 1803–11. Later additions include the clock and 6,000-pound bell in the cupola tower. The cupola itself is crowned with a stately, white-painted copper statue of *Justice* (anonymously produced in a workshop).

Barring days when there are demonstrations or special hearings that draw large crowds, you can enter the building between 10am and 4pm, Monday to Friday. Several areas are open to the public, beginning with the Corinthian-columned lobby, which centers on a coffered and skylit rotunda. The elegant Governor's Room upstairs, where Lafayette was received in 1824, houses a museum containing Washington's writing desk, his inaugural flag, and artwork by well-known American artists. This room is closed from noon to 1pm. City Hall contains quite an impressive collection of American art; in your wanderings, you might note works by George Caitlin, Thomas Sully, Samuel B. Morse, and Rembrandt Peale, among others.

☕ **Take a Break**   Grab a pastry or a diner meal at **Ellen's Café and Bake Shop,** 270 Broadway, at Chambers Street (☎ **212/962-1257**). Owner Ellen Hart won the Miss Subways beauty pageant in 1959, and her restaurant walls are lined with her own and other Miss Subways posters, plus photographs of all the politicians who eat here: Al D'Amato, Rudy Giuliani, Bella Abzug, Andy Stein, Mario Cuomo, and Geraldine Ferraro, to name just a few. Muffins, biscuits, and pastries are all oven fresh, and, of course, full breakfasts of eggs, bacon, pancakes, and Belgian waffles are available. Ellen's is open weekdays 6am to 7pm, Saturday 8am to 5pm; it's closed on Sunday.

Along the north edge of City Hall Park, on Chambers St., sits the now-shabby:

17. **Tweed Courthouse** (New York County Courthouse, 52 Chambers St.). This 1872 Italianate courthouse was built during the tenure of William Marcy "Boss" Tweed, who, in his post on the board of supervisors, stole millions in construction funds. Originally budgeted as a $250,000 job in 1861, the courthouse project escalated to the staggering sum of $14 million. Bills were padded to an unprecedented extent—Andrew Garvey, who was to become known as the "Prince of Plasterers," was paid $45,966.89 for a single day's work! The ensuing scandal (Tweed and his cronies, it came out, had pocketed at least $10 million) wrecked Tweed's career; he died penniless in jail.

Across Chambers St. and to the right, at the corner of Elk St., lies the turn-of-the-century:

18. **Surrogate's Court (The Hall of Records),** 31 Chambers St. Housed in this sumptuous beaux arts structure are all the legal records relating to Manhattan real estate deeds

and court cases, some dating from the mid-1600s. Heroic statues of distinguished New Yorkers (Peter Stuyvesant, De Witt Clinton, and others) front the mansard roof, and the doorways, surmounted by arched pediments, are flanked by Philip Martiny's sculptural groups portraying *New York in Revolutionary Times* (to your left) and *New York in Its Infancy* (to right). Above the entrance is a three-story Corinthian colonnade.

Step inside to see the vestibule's beautiful barrel-vaulted mosaic ceiling, embellished with astrological symbols, Egyptian and Greek motifs, and figures representing retribution, justice, sorrow, and labor. Continue back to the two-story skylit neoclassical atrium, clad in honey-colored marble with a colonnaded second-floor loggia and an ornate staircase adapted from the foyer of the Grand Opera House in Paris.

Exiting the Surrogate's Court from the front door, you'll see to your left, at the end of the block, that Chambers St. disappears under:

19. **The Municipal Building,** a grand civic edifice built between 1909 and 1914 to augment City Hall's government office space. It was designed by the famed architectural firm of McKim, Mead, and White (as in Stanford White), who used Greek and Roman design elements such as a massive Corinthian colonnade, ornately embellished vaults and cornices, and allegorical statuary. A triumphal arch, its barrel-vaulted ceiling adorned with relief panels, forms a magnificent arcade over Chambers Street; it has been called the "gate of the city." Sculptor Adolph Weinman created many of the building's bas-reliefs, medallions, and allegorical groupings of human figures (they symbolize civic pride, progress, guidance, prudence, and executive power). The heroic hammered-copper statue of Civic Fame, Manhattan's largest statue, that tops the structure 582 feet above the street was also designed by Weinman, holding a crown whose five turrets represent New York's five boroughs.

See many lovey-dovey couples walking in and out? The city's marriage license bureau is on the second floor, and a wedding takes place about every 20 minutes.

Chinatown

Start: The intersection of Broadway and Canal Street.
Subway: Take the 6, N, R, J, M, or Z to Canal Street.
Finish: The intersection of East Broadway and Rutgers Street.
Time: 3 to 4 hours, not including restaurant stops.
Best Time: Any time the weather is conducive to walking.

The main draw in Chinatown is the food; the neighborhood's 400-odd restaurants have satisfied New Yorkers' cravings for Cantonese, Hunan, and Szechuan fare, as well as Thai and Vietnamese cuisines for many years. But outside the doors of the restaurants, the swirling, exotic street life of one of the largest Chinese communities in the western hemisphere awaits. In the shops along Mott, Canal, and East Broadway, you'll find unusual foodstuff, Chinese herbal medicines, and collectibles that you'd think only a trip to Hong Kong or Shanghai could net. And you can also uncover in Chinatown's narrow streets and aging tenements, the legacies of immigrants—first the English, then the Germans, Irish, Italians, Jews, and finally, the Chinese.

Although East Indies trading ships brought handfuls of Chinese to New York from about 1840 on, it was not until the 1880s that Chinatown really began to develop. Thousands of Chinese sailed to California in the mid–19th century, hoping to

Chinatown

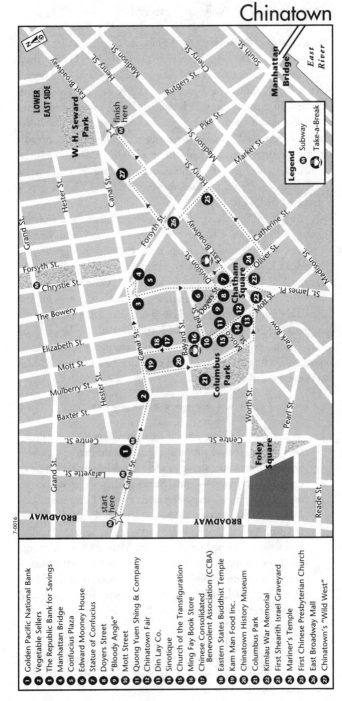

LOWER
EAST SIDE

W. H. Seward Park

finish here

Manhattan Bridge

East River

Legend
Ⓜ Subway
☕ Take-a-Break

Foley Square

BROADWAY

start here

❶ Golden Pacific National Bank
❷ Vegetable Sellers
❸ The Republic Bank for Savings
❹ Manhattan Bridge
❺ Confucius Plaza
❻ Edward Mooney House
❼ Statue of Confucius
❽ Doyers Street
❾ "Bloody Angle"
❿ Mott Street
⓫ Quong Yuen Shing & Company
⓬ Chinatown Fair
⓭ Din Lay Co.
⓮ Sinotique
⓯ Church of the Transfiguration
⓰ Ming Fay Book Store
⓱ Chinese Consolidated Benevolent Association (CCBA)
⓲ Eastern States Buddhist Temple
⓳ Kam Man Food Inc.
⓴ Chinatown History Museum
㉑ Columbus Park
㉒ Kimlau War Memorial
㉓ First Shearith Israel Graveyard
㉔ Mariner's Temple
㉕ First Chinese Presbyterian Church
㉖ East Broadway Mall
㉗ Chinatown's "Wild West"

amass fortunes by working the mines and building railroads, so they could return to China rich men. By the 1870s, they became the victims of a tide of racism, violence, and legal persecution throughout the West. In 1882, Congress passed the Chinese Exclusion Act, which denied Chinese the right to citizenship, barred them from most occupations, and suspended immigration. Additionally, the act forbade any laborers already in the country from bringing their wives here. Some Chinese returned home, but tens of thousands remained. From 1880 to 1890 the Chinese population on Mott, Pell, and Doyers streets increased tenfold to 12,000.

By the 1890s, Chinatown had become a large and isolated ghetto, and remained so for many years. Since World War II, however, the neighborhood has been building bridges to the American mainstream. A large influx of foreign capital from Taiwan and Hong Kong has helped make Chinatown one of New York's strongest local economies, and many Chinese Americans have joined the middle class. But unlike other famous immigrant neighborhoods such as Little Italy or the Lower East Side, Chinatown isn't ready to be relegated to the history books—immigrants from all parts of Asia continue to stream in, adding new energy and color.

• • • • • • • • • • • • • • • •

Start off walking east along **Canal Street.** You'll probably have to thread your way through a multiethnic throng of pedestrians and street vendors hawking toys, firecrackers, and dumplings—Canal Street during business hours is one of New York's most frenzied, crowded thoroughfares. From Broadway to the Bowery, Canal Street is lined with bustling variety stores, fish markets, greengrocers, banks, and Chinese-owned jewelry shops. Many of the storefronts have been subdivided into minimalls whose stalls purvey everything from ginseng to martial arts paraphernalia. However, when night falls and the shops are shuttered, Canal Street takes on the semblance of a ghost town in the hills of China.

Whatever time of day, you'll always see plenty of Chinese-language signs on Canal as soon as you walk east of Broadway, the landmark that signals your arrival in Chinatown proper is the former:

1. **Golden Pacific National Bank.** Located on the northwest corner of Canal and Centre streets, this building was
raised in 1983 as the bank's new home. At first a major
point of pride in the neighborhood, the bank failed only
2 years later and its patrons, largely individual Chinese, lost
their uninsured deposits. The colorful building, with a jade-
trimmed red pagoda roof and elaborately decorated facade
with Oriental phoenix and dragon motifs, has been resur-
rected as a busy jewelry exchange. Walk around on Centre
Street to see the building in its entirety.

  Although this one is defunct, Canal Street is still lined
with banks; indeed Chinatown's 161,000 residents are served
by several dozen of them, more than most cities of similar
size. Many Chinatown residents routinely put away 30%
to 50% of their wages.

  Continue east along Canal Street, and look for:

2. **Vegetable sellers** plying their trade on a traffic island at
Baxter Street. Here you can peruse and purchase Chinese
produce—bok choy (delicate Chinese cabbage), small white
and red-violet eggplants, taro root, fresh ginger, Chinese
squash, big white winter melons, tender bamboo shoots,
yard-long green beans, pale golden lily buds, lotus leaves,
cucumber-sized okras, and sweet snow peas. Cross from the
traffic island to the southern side of Canal Street where you'll
smell a briny aroma emanating from a **fish market** (no. 214)
whose crushed-ice–covered offerings spill well out onto the
sidewalk. The aproned fish sellers keep up a steady patter,
extolling the virtues of their shark, squid, snapper, oysters,
and eels. Here and throughout your tour, you'll also pass
carts vending Peking duck, chicken feet, roast pork, and lo
mein, as well as store windows displaying barbecued chickens, ducks, and squab with heads and beaks fully intact.

  Continue up Canal several more bustling, crowded
blocks, soaking up the street scene, to the southwest corner
of Canal Street and the Bowery (at 58 Bowery), where you'll
find a branch of the:

3. **The Republic Bank for Savings.** Built in 1924, and
later overhauled and tailored to its Chinese depositors, this
dome-roofed bank is one of New York's most distinctive.
(It's hard to appreciate from directly underneath; cross Canal

for a better view). Its interior is decorated with several dozen Ching dynasty paintings, some of them displayed in carved and gilded rosewood screens. A red and gold pagoda houses the bank's coffers, and the walls are lined with Chinese proverbs, which translate to: "Wealth comes from saving your money," and "If you're filthy rich, you're born with it; moderate wealth requires hard work." Other panels wish good luck and advise thoughtful consideration for others.

Across the Bowery to the east is the approach to the:

4. **Manhattan Bridge.** This suspension bridge, built in 1905, may not be as inspirational to poets and artists as the great Brooklyn Bridge, but the monumental beaux arts colonnade and arch that stand at its entrance are quite grand and arresting.

Looming to the right of the bridge, on the east side of the Bowery, is:

5. **Confucius Plaza.** The first major public-funded housing project built for Chinese use, Confucius Plaza extends from Division Street up to the Bowery where it rises into a curved 43-story tower.

The activist spirit of the 1960s touched Chinatown in a significant way: many neighborhood youths were involved in a Chinese-American pride movement and created organizations devoted to building community centers, providing social services, and securing Chinatown a voice in city government. Winning the fight to build this plaza and forcing contractors to hire Chinese workers showed that Chinatown was now a political heavy hitter.

Walk south on the Bowery to building no. 18, which sits on the southeast corner of the Bowery and Pell Street, and is called the:

6. **Edward Mooney House** (occupied by Summit Mortgage Bankers). This largely Georgian brick row house, painted red with beige trim, dates from George Washington's New York days. It was built in 1785 on property abandoned by a Tory who fled during the revolution, and is the oldest such house in the city.

The Bowery ends at Chatham Square, into which nine other streets converge. To your left on a traffic island you'll see the:

7. **Statue of Confucius.** Raised in 1976, this bronze statue and its green marble base were a gift of the Chinese Consolidated Benevolent Association (CCBA), which has served as Chinatown's unofficial government for more than 100 years. The organization has always represented conservative Chinese who support traditional notions of family loyalty and respect for one's elders and leaders; the statue was built over the strenuous objections of activist groups that felt the neighborhood should display a more progressive cultural symbol. However, the sage's 2,400-year-old words, inscribed in the monument's base in both Chinese and English, are strikingly descriptive of the strength of Chinatown's tight-knit social fabric: Confucius recommends that we look beyond our immediate family and see all our elders as our parents, and all children as our own.

From the statue of Confucius, follow Catherine Street past the pagoda-roofed Republic Bank for Savings, and turn left onto East Broadway. This thoroughfare is now the heart of commercial, workday Chinatown. Very few of its businesses are geared to tourists; instead, they are dedicated to serving the community's needs. There are Chinese video stores, beauty salons, sidewalk shacks purveying grilled meats and dumplings, and bakeries whose wedding cakes are topped with Asian bride and groom figurines.

☕ **Take a Break** For lunch, treat yourself to dim sum (see box below). Every day from 8am to about 4pm, two huge restaurants—the **Golden Unicorn** at 18 East Broadway; (☎ **212/941-0911**) and the **Nice Restaurant** at 35 East Broadway (☎ **212/406-9510**)—draw large, hungry crowds. The Golden Unicorn's walkie-talkie–wielding hostess directs incoming diners to the restaurant's second- and third-floor dining rooms; in the Nice Restaurant, the lobby has several tanks full of carp and sea bass. Usually you'll be seated with other parties around a huge banquet table. Once settled, you'll see that there's a distinctly celebratory spirit pervading the place; the Chinese families dining here often seem to have three or four generations represented. Help yourself—you can afford to take some risks since everything costs just $2 to $4 (prices at Nice are a tad lower than Golden Unicorn's). Though servers seldom speak much English, fellow Chinese diners or inveterate dim summers at your table might be able to offer some helpful tips.

Dim Sum

Dim sum is Cantonese for "dot your heart," and a dim sum meal consists of one small gastronomic delight after another. Simply choose what looks appealing from the steaming carts that servers wheel around to your table. Dim sum usually involves more than 100 appetizer-sized items—perhaps steamed leek dumplings, deep-fried minced shrimp rolls wrapped in bacon, sweet doughy buns filled with tangy morsels of barbecued pork, deep-fried shrimp, beef ribs with black pepper sauce, honey roast pork rolled in steamed noodles, and much more. There are dessert dim sum as well, such as orange pudding, egg custard rolls covered with shredded coconut, and sweet lotus-seed sesame balls.

Backtrack to Chatham Square. At the Bowery, on the square, a narrow, crooked street bears off to the northwest (in the general direction of Canal Street). This is:

8. **Doyers Street,** which along with Pell Street and the lower end of Mott Street formed the original Chinatown. Doyers was the backdrop for much of the neighborhood's unhappy early history.

Chinatown's "bachelor society," which existed from 1882 to 1943 (when some provisions of the Exclusion Act were repealed), was a place of grimly limited opportunity and deep poverty. There were 27 men to every woman in the neighborhood. These men were prohibited from competing with whites for work, hemmed into Chinatown by the language barrier, and living under the risk of beatings if they strayed from the three-block ghetto. Under these harsh conditions, working in the laundry industry was one of the best ways to eke out a living.

Crime compounded the neighborhood's misery. The Chinese moved into the northern end of an area that for

40 years had been a sprawling morass of saloons, gambling dens, and squalid tenements extending from Chatham Square all the way to the waterfront. Prostitution flourished (out of desperation, many Chinese men lived with, or even married, white prostitutes) and opium dens sprang up. The Chinese Consolidated Benevolent Association (CCBA) acted as de facto government, but real power resided in the *tongs,* protection societies involved in racketeering and gambling. There are still tong-controlled gaming dens in Chinatown, still whispers of intimidation, and an occasional outbreak of gang-related violence.

The post office located a few paces up Doyers Street on your right now occupies the site of the old Chatham Club, one of the uproarious music halls that surrounded Chatham Square a century ago. The clubs boasted singing waiters, accompanied by a tinny piano, who would entertain the clientele with sentimental ballads. Izzy Baline and Al Yoelson sang at the Chatham and other clubs on Doyers; later, in tonier surroundings, they became better known as Irving Berlin and Al Jolson.

By the 1920s, the sharp bend in Doyers Street had acquired its reputation as the infamous:

9. **"Bloody Angle."** The first two tongs to rise in Chinatown, the On Leong and the Hip Sing, engaged in a fierce turf struggle in Chinatown that dragged on for almost 40 years. Both organizations had large standing armies of henchmen, and the worst of the continual bloodshed occurred here. The crooked street lent itself to ambush, and assassins could usually make a fast escape by ducking through the old Chinese Theatre, which stood at the elbow of the street that the Viet-Nam restaurant now occupies. At the turn of the century, Bloody Angle was the site of more murders than anywhere else in the United States.

At the end of Doyers is Pell Street, another short, narrow thoroughfare lined with restaurants that has changed little over the years. At no. 16 is the unobtrusive entryway to the headquarters of the organization that has dominated Pell and Doyers streets for 100 years, the Hip Sing tong, its gold lettering above the door symbolizing growth and prosperity.

Leaving the dark side of the neighborhood's history behind, turn left on Pell down to its intersection with:

10. **Mott Street,** the heart of old Chinatown. Mott is the epi-center of the boisterous Chinese New Year celebrations that begin with the first full moon after January 21—red and gold streamers festoon every shop window and the street fills with parades complete with gyrating dragon dancers and the nonstop thunder of firecrackers.

    The shops that line Mott Street are a diverse bunch, and collectively their stock gives you the chance to bring a piece of Chinatown back home. Just around the corner to your left is one such store:

11. **Quong Yuen Shing & Company,** at 32 Mott St. The oldest store in Chinatown, Quong Yuen Shing celebrated its 100th birthday in 1991. It has changed remarkably little—the tin ceiling, hanging scales, and the decorative panels in the back above the ornately framed counter (over which Chinese herbal medicines were once dispensed) all keep the place looking just as it did in the 1890s. Along with sandalwood fans, tea and mah-jongg sets, ceramic bowls and vases, and seeds for Chinese vegetables, the store still sells merchandise it's been stocking for a century. One such item is silk handkerchiefs, which Chinatown laundries would once buy and pass on to their best customers at Christmastime.

    Continue along Mott Street to the:

12. **Chinatown Fair,** at 8 Mott St. Tucked in between the familiar video game machines, you'll find vintage pinball games and other arcade antiques like the Luv-O-Meter and the test-your-strength machine. A glass-enclosed booth houses a chicken that is proclaimed a master of electronic tic-tac-toe (you supposedly win a large bag of fortune cookies if you beat her, but the chicken's consummate skill has kept me from verifying this).

    Across Mott is the:

13. **Din Lay Co.,** at 5 Mott St. An old, slightly musty shop, Din Lay is worth a visit for its unbeatable collection of classic Chinatown souvenirs—there are mah-jongg sets and tables, incense burners, joss sticks, tea sets, delicate

rice-paper fans and stationery, sandalwood-scented soap, stainless-steel balls to roll in your hand, and much more.

A few doors up to the north is:

14. **Sinotique,** at 19a Mott St. Inside this refined, decidedly upscale shop you'll find beautiful, high-quality Chinese antiques, crafts, and collectibles. On a recent visit, these included rosewood and teak cabinets with delicate hand-carved ornamentation; pottery ranging from unglazed pieces created in the 2nd millennium B.C. through the Ching dynasty; exquisite carved bamboo birdcages from southern China (ask them to explain the traditional bird-keeping hobby common among old Chinese men); Chinese country furniture; Tibetan, Chinese, and Mongolian rugs; hand-wrought mounted bronze gongs, and jewelry.

Cross tiny Mosco Street and you'll be in front of the:

15. **Church of the Transfiguration,** at 25–29 Mott St. This Georgian stone church was built in 1801; the spire was added in the 1860s. Originally consecrated as the English Lutheran First Church of Zion, Transfiguration has been a veritable chameleon reflecting the changing image of the neighborhood. It was created as a house of worship for English Lutherans, then for the newly arrived Irish Catholics, and later, in the 1880s, the Italian Catholics. Nowadays its services are in Cantonese and Mandarin, and the church is the focal point of New York's Chinese Roman Catholic community. Transfiguration remains true to its long heritage as a mission house, continuing to offer English classes and other services that help its members find their way into the American mainstream.

Take a Break Just beyond Pell Street is the **New Lung Fong Bakery,** 41 Mott St. (☎ 212/233-7447), offering an array of sweet treats such as red-bean cakes, black-bean doughnuts, custard tarts, chestnut buns, cream buns, melon cakes, and mixed-nut pies. Sitting in Lung Fong's unadorned cafe section, you can relax with a cup of tea or very good coffee and *yum cha*—that's Chinese for hanging out, talking, and drinking in a cafe.

Continue north on Mott. On the right at 42 Mott St. is the:

16. **Ming Fay Book Store.** An eclectic store stocked with everything from art/school supplies and toys to Chinese calendars, newspapers, comics, pinup magazines, and books, Ming Fay also carries a selection of English-language books on Chinese subjects. A sampling of titles: *Chinese Astrology, The Bruce Lee Story, The Book of Tea, The Dictionary of Traditional Chinese Medicine,* and *The Living Buddha.*

Just past the bookstore is a permanent food stall that sells nothing but fried white-radish cakes, and a little farther up Mott at no. 62 is the headquarters of the:

17. **Chinese Consolidated Benevolent Association (CCBA).** Until recently, it functioned as the working government of Chinatown, helping new immigrants find jobs and housing, funneling capital into neighborhood businesses, offering English classes to children and adults, providing services to the elderly, and even operating criminal courts. While its influence has waned somewhat, it is still a major social and political force in Chinatown, and is the voice of New York's pro-Taiwan community. Also located in the building is the Chinese School, which since 1915 has been working to keep the Chinese traditions and language alive, long a primary concern of the CCBA.

Two doors down is the:

18. **Eastern States Buddhist Temple of America.** This storefront shrine has been here for years. Quiet and suffused with incense, it serves as something of a social center; there are usually a number of elderly ladies sitting in the chairs and benches that line the wall. Enter, light a joss stick, and offer a prayer to Kuan Yin, the Chinese goddess of mercy. Or perhaps you'd rather supplicate the Four-Faced Buddha for good luck in business (money will come from all directions, hence the four faces). You can also buy a fortune here, in English, for a dollar.

Across the street, near the corner of Mott and Canal (83–85 Mott), behind a stately facade that includes balconies and a pagoda roof, is the headquarters of the **Chinese Merchants Association,** better known as On Leong. This is Chinatown's oldest *tong* and still one of its most prominent neighborhood organizations.

Make a left onto Canal Street, where a steady stream of shoppers will no doubt be passing in and out of:

19. **Kam Man Food Inc.** at 200 Canal St. This quintessential Chinese supermarket makes for a truly fascinating browse. To your right as you enter is a selection of elaborately packaged teas and elixirs laced with ginseng and other mainstays of Chinese pharmacopoeia. These include tzepao sanpien extract (which promises greater potency to men), heart tonics, stop-smoking and slimming teas, deer-tail extract, edible bird's nests, tiger liniment, and royal jelly. Many, such as *bu tian su*—good for memory loss, insomnia, an aching back, or lumbago, among other things— claim to cure a wide variety of ailments. Just beyond this collection is a counter displaying myriad varieties of ginseng. Walk toward the rear of the store and you'll find packages of pork buns ready for the steamer, quail eggs, dried seafood, exotic mushrooms, sauces ranging from oyster to black-bean garlic, a butcher section, and much more. Downstairs, the kitchenware department offers everything from woks to tea sets, and a counter for fancy chopsticks, roasted seaweed, and oodles of noodles. Pick up some essence of tienchi flowers, a purported remedy for pimples, dizziness, hot temper, grinding of teeth, and emotional inquietude.

    Turn left onto Mulberry Street (another thoroughfare lined with emporia that make for great browsing and window shopping), to visit the:

20. **Chinatown History Museum,** 70 Mulberry St. (☎ 212/ 619-4785). In the forward-looking, upwardly mobile climate of today's Chinatown, not many want to think about the cruel hardships that the first generations of Chinese in New York suffered. This museum, founded in 1980, documents the history and culture of Chinese in America from the early 1800s to the present. An adjoining gallery stages exhibitions of works by Chinese artists and photographers, and there's a gift/book store. Hours are Tuesday to Thursday and Saturday noon to 5pm; they charge a small admission.

    Opening off to the southwest on the other side of Mulberry Street is:

21. **Columbus Park.** Open public spaces are in short supply on the Lower East Side, and the dingy but lively Columbus Park is popular with Chinatown residents both young and old. Here old Chinese women play cards for dimes or have

their fortunes told, while, in another area, Chinese men gamble over checkers. The park lies where a huddle of decrepit tenements known as Mulberry Bend once stood. In the last quarter of the 19th century, Mulberry Bend was New York's worst slum, as evinced by the frightening nomenclature it acquired—the filthy tenements went by names such as Bone Alley, Kerosene Row, and Bandits' Roost. Such brawling street gangs as the Dead Rabbits, Plug Uglies, and Whyos were the powers of Mulberry Bend, and police only ventured into the area in platoons of 10 or more.

Mulberry Bend remained New York's disgrace until social reformer Jacob Riis managed to stir up public rage to the point where city officials were obliged to raze the slum between 1892 and 1894. For the last century, Riis's vision of a clean place for neighborhood children to play in has become a reality—there's a big playground and games of basketball, baseball, or hockey are almost always in progress.

At the southern end of the park, make a left turn onto Worth Street and you'll soon be back at Chatham Square. Up ahead on your right on the traffic island is the:

22. **Kimlau War Memorial,** built in 1962 to honor the Chinese Americans who gave their lives while serving in the U.S. armed forces. Chinatown's extraordinary contribution to the American war effort in World War II—40% of the neighborhood's population served in the military—was a major factor in the annulment of the Chinese Exclusion Act and other anti-Chinese legislation.

St. James Place, which extends south from Chatham Square, is the site of the:

23. **First Shearith Israel Graveyard,** a burial ground for Sephardic Jews who emigrated to New York in the mid–17th century. The 1683 stone of Benjamin Bueno de Mesquita (still legible) is the oldest in the city; the cemetery remained active until 1828 and features the graves of a number of soldiers who died during the American Revolution. Also buried here, in 1733, is Rachel Rodriguez Marques, an ancestor of New York stockbroker, politico, and college benefactor Bernard Baruch (who paid for the improvement of the site in the 1950s). The gate is usually locked, but you can peer through the fence.

Backtrack on St. James Place, and turn right onto Oliver Street. On the northeast corner of Oliver and Henry streets is the:

24. **Mariner's Temple.** This Greek Revival brownstone church, with a portico entranceway fronted by two massive Ionic columns, was built in 1844. Today a Baptist church serving a mixed Chinese, African American, and Latino congregation, the Mariner's Temple originally catered to the sea captains, dockworkers, and sailors of the sprawling maritime community that dominated the waterfront along the East River in the 19th century.

Turn left onto Henry Street. Two blocks east, on the corner of Henry and Market streets, is the:

25. **First Chinese Presbyterian Church,** which shares a place in neighborhood history with the Mariner's Temple. Built in 1819 on the outskirts of the Cherry Hill section (which after the Revolutionary War was New York's poshest neighborhood and the site of the nation's first presidential mansion), this Georgian-style house of worship was originally named the Northeast Dutch Reformed Church. It was renamed the Church of Sea and Land during the mid–19th century, when the East River waterfront had become rife with cutthroat saloons, dance halls, and "crimps"—lodging houses that often took advantage of their sailor patrons by robbing them or even shanghaiing them aboard outgoing ships. Mission houses like the Mariner's Temple and the Church of Sea and Land were often the only place to which beleaguered seafarers and immigrants could turn for help. Today, the church continues to assist the immigrants who arrive in Chinatown in droves every year.

Turn left and follow Market Street to bustling East Broadway and turn right. Believe it or not, the dim, noisy area below the Manhattan Bridge is a commercial hot spot of Chinatown. On your left is the modest:

26. **East Broadway Mall.** The stores cater entirely to Chinese shoppers and include a newsstand at which you'll be lucky to spot a word of English, a Chinese pop music shop, two Chinese-language video stores, several beauty salons and cosmetics shops selling products you won't find in your

average beauty store, and Ho's Ginseng Co., where you can get something to cool down your blood (or warm it up). The mall's centerpiece is a glitzy upstairs restaurant, the Triple Eight Palace.

Continue along East Broadway, and you'll soon cross Pike Street. Pike is an unofficial divider between the established area of Chinatown and an expanding area that's been termed:

27. **Chinatown's "Wild West"** by journalist Gwen Kinkead in her book *Chinatown: A Portrait of a Closed Society* (HarperCollins, 1992). Asians have been flooding into New York City ever since U.S. immigration laws were liberalized in 1965. The great majority of them hail from the People's Republic of China, and most of these new immigrants come from Fujian Province, often via Hong Kong or Taiwan. These new arrivals have almost completely replaced the old immigrant residents of the Lower East Side, the Jews. Emblematic of the changing makeup in the neighborhood is the **Sons of Israel Kalwarie Synagogue,** located on Pike Street to the right of East Broadway—it's now a Buddhist association.

Walk down East Broadway to Rutgers Street (where you'll find the entrance to the subway's East Broadway F-line stop). The Chinatown you'll pass on your way may not have curio shops or pagoda roofs, but the barber shops, fish markets, and newsstands do a brisk business. All throughout this neighborhood, you'll see hectic commerce, hardworking laborers, schoolchildren, and you can sense the buzz of a neighborhood whose people are working to leave these gritty tenement streets and make their way into the mainstream, just as people on the Lower East Side have been doing for more than a century.

The Jewish
Lower East Side

Start: Bialystoker Synagogue, 7 Bialystoker Place.

Subway: Take the F train to Delancy Street, or the J, M, or Z to Essex Street.

Finish: Russ and Daughters, 179 Houston St.

Time: Approximately 3½ to 4 hours if you do all the tours.

Best Time: Sundays, when you can tour the Eldridge Street Synagogue (Stop 6) and see Orchard Street in full form. If you begin around 9:30am, you'll also get a chance to look inside Bialystoker Synagogue (Stop 1). *Note:* Since tours of the highly recommended Lower East Side Tenement Museum sometimes fill up on Sundays, you might want to stop there earlier in the day (it opens at 11am) and pick up tickets; see details below (Stop 11).

Worst Time: Saturdays and Jewish holidays when almost everything is closed; Friday afternoons, when stores close early.

The Lower East Side has always been one of New York's most colorful neighborhoods. More than 23 million Europeans emigrated to American shores between 1880 and 1919, seeking escape from famine, poverty, and religious persecution. About 1.5 million Jews, many of them fleeing Russian pogroms, wound up in ramshackle tenements here. They scratched out meager livings peddling wares on Orchard Street or working dawn to dusk in garment center sweatshops. By 1920, some 500 synagogues and religious schools (talmud torahs) dotted the area. Though the garment center has moved uptown, and the ethnic mix is different today, Orchard Street, the area's primary shopping artery, and its immediate surroundings remain a largely Orthodox Jewish enclave. And the area is rich in Jewish history; 80% of today's American Jews are descendants of immigrants who once lived on these streets. Today, there are more Jews in New York—almost 2 million—than anywhere else in the world outside of Israel.

Food Note: This is an eating tour as well as a walking tour as there's great noshing along the way.

• • • • • • • • • • • • • • • •

Starting Out **Ratner's Dairy Restaurant,** 138 Delancey St., between Norfolk and Suffolk streets (☎ 212/677-5588), is the oldest Jewish dairy restaurant in the city. People have been coming here since 1905 (first on Grand Street, then, at the present location since 1917) to feast on cheese and berry blintzes smothered in sour cream, kreplach, gefilte fish (the way Grandma used to make it), whitefish salad, potato latkes, and matzo brei. Ratner's has always been popular with New York politicos wooing the Jewish vote. Former Gov. Nelson Rockefeller always ate here the night before elections; he said it was good luck. And during the 1989 Democratic mayoral primary, rival candidates David Dinkins and Ed Koch were surprised to run into each other at breakfast one morning; they civilly shook hands and proceeded to devour bagels and lox. All breads and cakes are baked on the premises. A basket of scrumptious onion rolls accompanies every meal, and there are great desserts (try the strawberry cheesecake or chocolate cream pie). Open Sunday to Thursday 6am to 8:30pm, Friday 6am to 3pm, Saturday sundown to 2am.

Many Lower East Side kosher restaurants have recently began transforming into night clubs after hours to blend into the new funky attitude taking over this neighborhood. The Lansky Lounge, Ratner's after-dark alter ego, is open

The Jewish Lower East Side

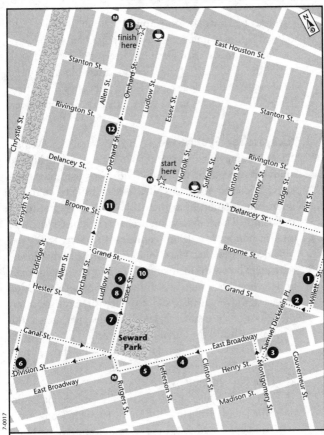

1. Bialystoker Synagogue
2. Abrons Arts Center/Harry De Jur Playhouse
3. The Henry Street Settlement
4. Educational Alliance
5. Forward Building
6. Eldridge Street Synagogue
7. Weinfeld's Skull Cap Mfg.
8. Essex Street Pickles
9. Hebrew Religious Articles
10. Kossar's Bialys
11. Lower East Side Tenement Museum Orientation Center
12. Orchard Street
13. Russ and Daughters

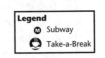

Legend

Ⓜ Subway

☕ Take-a-Break

Saturday to Thursday from around 8:30pm until 4 or 5am (closed Saturday mid-May though early October).

From Ratner's, cross Delancey Street; turn left and walk down the south side of the street for a few blocks, around to the right of the bridge ramp. Take a right onto Bialystoker Place/Willet Street. On the right, just past Broome Street, is the:

1. **Bialystoker Synagogue,** 7 Bialystoker Place (Willett Street). Occupying a converted 1826 Federal-style fieldstone church, this beautiful Orthodox landsmanschaft shul (synagogue of countrymen) was purchased in 1905 by an immigrant congregation from Bialystok (then in Russia, today in Poland). The congregation itself was organized in 1878, and, in honor of its 100th anniversary, Willett Street was renamed Bialystoker Place in 1978. Enter via the downstairs steps below the main doors. The temple's interior walls and ceiling are ornately painted with Moorish motifs, zodiac signs (which are found in the Jewish scriptural interpretations of the cabbalah), and biblical scenes such as the Wailing Wall and the burial place of Rachel. The elaborate gold-leafed ark was designed in Italy. Look up at the glittering crystal chandeliers, which hang from a ceiling painted as a blue sky with fluffy white clouds.

Bialystoker Synagogue is open daily (except for Saturdays, the Jewish Sabbath) until about 10:30am (sometimes later) and evenings (except for Fridays) from 6:30 to 8pm; if you're going at another time, you can call a day or two ahead (☎ 475-0165) to arrange admission.

Continue up Willets Street and make a right onto Grand Street. The modern, curvilinear brick building on your right is the modern extension of the:

2. **Abrons Arts Center/Harry De Jur Playhouse,** 466 Grand St. (☎ 212/598-0400). Founded by sisters Alice and Irene Lewisohn in 1915 to stage productions of the Henry Street Settlement's youthful dramatic groups, this renowned center went on to present premieres of S. Ansky's *The Dybbuk* (attended by authors Edna Ferber and Willa Cather) and James Joyce's *Exiles,* along with plays by George Bernard Shaw, Havelock Ellis, Anton Chekhov, Scholem Asch, and Eugene O'Neill. It remains a vital performance

space and cultural center, offering a comprehensive schedule of dance, theater, music, art exhibits, classes, and workshops. Pick up an events schedule while you're here. Behind this modern extension, is the center's original core, a three-story Georgian Revival building.

Cross Grand and head left down Samuel Dickstein Plaza. It runs into the intersection of Henry and Montgomery streets; take a sharp left onto Henry Street, and immediately on your left is:

3. **The Henry Street Settlement,** 263–267 Henry St. Called to tend a patient on Ludlow Street in 1892, 25-year-old German-Jewish nurse Lillian Wald was appalled at the squalor of tenement life. She moved downtown in order to study conditions in the Jewish ghetto, and, in 1893, established a district nursing service on Henry Street. Two years later, it evolved into the Henry Street Settlement, one of America's first social agencies, offering job training, educational facilities, summer camps for children, concerts, and plays.

Wald dedicated her life to helping the indigent of the Lower East Side fight disease, malnutrition, and ignorance, and the "house on Henry Street" initiated progressive social legislation, including child labor laws. Social reformer Jacob Riis said of her, "From the very start, the poor became 'her people.' She took them to her heart and they quickly gave her unstinted love and trust." Years ago you might have seen Jane Addams, Albert Einstein, or Eleanor Roosevelt discussing vital social issues in the dining room. Pres. Bill Clinton visited during his 1992 campaign. The settlement continues its good works, operating homeless shelters and numerous programs for neighborhood residents. Its three original late-Federal buildings, today used only for administrative purposes, are designated landmarks.

Turn around and head back to the corner, where you make a right back up Montgomery Street (through the small cement park) toward the high rise apartments, and take a left into East Broadway. A ways down on your left is the:

4. **Educational Alliance (the David Sarnoff Building),** 197 East Broadway. The Alliance was founded in 1889 by "uptown" German-Jewish philanthropists to help fellow immigrants assimilate, Americanize, and adapt to a baffling

alien culture. It offered them training in English, courses in business, cultural and civic programs, legal counsel, music lessons, and athletic facilities, not to mention such hard-to-come-by amenities as hot showers and pasteurized milk for children.

Today, the Educational Alliance's programs operate out of 21 locations and serve not only Jews, but black, Chinese, and Latin American New Yorkers. A Hall of Fame on the main floor is lined with photos of notable alumni such as Eddie Cantor, David Sarnoff, Jan Peerce, Jacob Epstein, Arthur Murray, and Louise Nevelson.

Continue in the same direction. You'll notice by the signs that the old Jewish neighborhood here has given way to the ever-expanding and vibrant Chinese neighborhood, which far exceeds the traditional boundaries that maps label "Chinatown." At 175 East Broadway, you'll see the tall old:

5. **Forward Building.** For 60 years, this was the home of America's most prominent Yiddish newspaper. Founded in 1897 by a group of Russian Jewish immigrants, the *Forverts* guided thousands of Eastern European Jews through the confusing maze of American society. In the 1920s, its daily circulation reached 250,000 copies.

Lithuanian immigrant Abraham Cahan served as editor from the newspaper's inception until his death in 1951. Under his guidance, this socialist and zealously prolabor newspaper examined every facet of Jewish and American life. It explained American customs and social graces to greenhorns—everything from baseball to personal hygiene—and exhorted readers to learn English and educate their children. The paper also presented—along with trashy serialized romance novels—quality fiction by writers like Sholem Asch, Sholem Aleichem, I.J. Singer, and I.B. Singer. Singer worked on staff throughout his adult life, and all his books, which were written in Yiddish (later translated) were always first published in *The Forward.*

Today the Forward building, constructed in 1912 specifically to house the paper, is a Chinese-American community center. Though the male and female figures centered on a sunburst above the door remain (they symbolize enlightenment), the flaming torches (socialist symbols) and portraits of Marx and Engels on the building's facade are obscured by Chinese signage. But, *The Forward* still exists today as a vital newspaper headquartered uptown. Since 1990, it has published in English as well as in Yiddish.

In the heyday of the *Forverts,* the Chinese restaurant now occupying the corner of Rutgers Street and East Broadway was the Garden Cafeteria—a superb dairy restaurant patronized by members of the Jewish intelligentsia; Leon Trotsky frequently dined here when he was in New York.

From Rutgers Street, make a left on Canal Street, bear left onto Division Street, and make a right on Eldridge Street to the:

6. **Eldridge Street Synagogue** (Congregation K'hal Adath Jeshurun, 12–16 Eldridge St.; ☎ **212/219-0888**). When it was built in 1886 by a congregation of Polish and Russian Jews, this was the most magnificent of the Lower East Side's temples. It was also the first synagogue built by Eastern European immigrants, who had previously worshipped in converted churches. Designed by the Herter Brothers (interior designers for wealthy New York families like the Vanderbilts), its architectural and interior decor reflects a blend of Gothic, Romanesque, and Moorish styles. The grandiose terra-cotta and brick facade is highly symbolic: Its cluster of five small windows represent the five books of Moses, the 12 roundels of the rose window symbolize the 12 tribes of Israel, and so on. The highly deteriorated, but once opulent, sanctuary was fitted out under a 70-foot central dome with an ornately carved towering walnut ark from Italy, trompe l'oeil murals, stained-glass windows, scagliola columns, and Victorian glass-shaded brass chandeliers.

The congregation flourished for several decades, but as wealthy members moved away, and quota laws of the 1920s slowed immigration to a trickle, funds became short and the building deteriorated. By the 1940s the main sanctuary was in such bad repair it was boarded up. Not until the 1970s did urban preservationists and historians begin taking an interest. The Eldridge Street Project, founded in 1986, is now restoring it as an active synagogue and Jewish heritage center. The temple has a small Orthodox congregation.

Visitors can take 1-hour tours every Sunday on the hour from 11am to 4pm, Tuesday and Thursday at 11:30am and 2:30pm, or by appointment. Admission is charged (it goes toward the renovation). While you're here, inquire about the temple's many programs, lectures, and neighborhood walking tours.

From the synagogue, make a right on Canal Street and a left on Essex Street, where you'll find many fascinating little shops carrying Judaica, kosher foods, and religious articles.

7. **Weinfeld's Skull Cap Mfg.,** at 19 Essex St., is a century-old yarmulke factory run by succeeding generations of Weinfelds. Yarmulkes are small skullcaps used by Orthodox Jewish men. They also make *tallith* (fringed prayer shawls worn by men during Jewish religious services), prayer book bags, and tallith bags.

Continue uptown to:

8. **Essex Street Pickles** (better known as Guss Pickle Products), 35 Essex St. (☎ **800/252-4877**), which was featured in the movie *Crossing Delancey.* You'll smell the shop's briny aroma halfway down the street. Guss's originated in 1910, and it's now in the fourth generation. The giant plastic barrels that line the sidewalk out front are filled with sours, half sours, hot pickles, pickled tomatoes, olives, sauerkraut, horseradish, and other delicacies. Everything is made on the premises. Buy a delicious pickle to eat on the street, or purchase a jar full. They're open Sunday to Thursday 9am to 6pm, Friday 9am to 4pm.

Just up the block is:

9. **Hebrew Religious Articles,** at 45 Essex St. (☎ **212/ 674-1770**). The shop has been here for more than 50 years. Its shelves and display cases are cluttered with Jewish books, ritual phylacteries and shawls, sacred scrolls, commentaries on the Torah, menorahs, antique Judaica, electric memorial candles, seder plates, mezuzahs, yarmulkes, cantorial and Yiddish records, and a marvelous collection of turn-of-the-century Eastern European postcards.

Make a right on Grand Street to:

10. **Kossar's Bialys,** 367 Grand St., where you can watch bakers making bialys, bagels, and *bulkas* (long bialylike rolls). Bialys—round rolls with a dimple in the middle—were invented by bakers from the Polish town of Bialystok, and this shop has been making delicious ones since the turn of the century.

Backtrack west along Grand Street, crossing Essex, and make a right onto Orchard Street. At Broome, you'll come to the orientation center for the:

11. **Lower East Side Tenement Museum,** 90 Orchard St. (☎ 212/431-0233). Conceived as a monument to the experience of "urban pioneers" in America, this unique facility documents the lives of immigrant residents in an 1863 six-story, 22-apartment tenement: 97 Orchard St., accessible only via the highly recommended guided tour.

The orientation center/gift shop is where you buy tour tickets and can view a 28-minute orientation video. You will also find a two-sided, glass-walled, dollhouse-like model of 97 Orchard St. here. Based on records and research into the individual families that once lived in the building, this mock-up shows the activities of actual residents on a morning in 1870 (on one side) and on a morning in 1915 (on another). All of the furnishings and settings are marvelously realistic, and some of the doll's faces were created with the aid of photographs to resemble actual tenants. Tenants are depicted preparing for Passover, doing sweatshop labor, writing letters home, dealing with illness, reading the *Forverts,* even using the chamber pot. Also on display here are Depression-era photographs of tenement life by Hungarian-born WPA artist Arnold Eagle and some of the 1,500 objects found in nooks and crannies of the building.

The guided tour gives a thorough history, but to whet your appetite, here are a few quick facts about the building: Up to 10,000 people from 20 different countries lived at 97 Orchard over a period of 72 years (the landlord sealed the building up in 1935 so he wouldn't have to bring it up to code under the new housing laws—inadvertently creating the perfect time capsule). These immigrants probably would have been astonished to hear that their crowded building of cold, cramped, airless apartments would one day be listed on the National Register of Historic Landmarks.

Residents lived (and often worked, sewing piece work for garment manufacturers or taking in laundry) in three-room apartments with a total area of just 325 square feet. Scant light trickled through windows at distant ends of railroad flats, and the only heat came from the coal- or wood-burning cooking stove. Large families, often supplemented by boarders for extra cash, lived in such dwellings without running water (until the 1890s it had to be fetched from a backyard pump and hauled upstairs). Other modern conveniences that tenants had to do without included indoor plumbing (until plumbing was installed at the turn of the century, chamber pots served as toilets and slops had to be carried to privies in the backyard; after that there were toilets in the hall), and electricity (which may not have been installed until the 1920s). Bed legs were often placed in cans of kerosene, which, though it created a fire hazard, discouraged bedbugs. Lucas Glockner, the German immigrant who built the place, was unhampered by building codes; few existed at the time, and even they were not enforced. By 1915, as many as 18 people sometimes occupied one apartment, sleeping in shifts. In such unhealthy conditions, 40% of the babies born here died, and disease was rampant. The museum has re-created two apartments inside, based on records, letters, and the memories of people who once lived here as children, and is working on a third.

The museum is open Tuesday to Friday noon to 5pm, Saturday and Sunday 11am to 5pm. There is an admission for the 1-hour tours, which take place Tuesday to Friday at 1, 2, and 3pm, Saturday and Sunday every 45 minutes between 11am and 5pm (last tour at 4:15). Pick up a schedule of the museum's weekend neighborhood tours for future excursions.

Continue up the block, crossing Delancey Street to enter the shop-lined stretch of:

12. **Orchard Street.** It's hard to imagine, but Orchard Street was named for the orchards of an 18th-century farm at this location owned by James Delancey, lieutenant governor of the British province of New York (Delancey Street is named for him). In the 19th century it was a vast outdoor marketplace, with rows of pushcarts lining both sides of the street.

Today, pushcarts have been replaced by stores, though much of the merchandise is still displayed outside on racks. This is bargain shopping. You can save up to 50% over uptown department stores here, and many shop owners are willing to haggle over prices. However, don't expect polite service. Sundays the street is so jammed with shoppers that it is closed to vehicular traffic between Delancey and Houston streets. But Orchard Street on Sunday is a phenomenon you must experience at least once. Come back to do serious shopping on a weekday when you have the stores to yourself.

Continue north on Orchard Street, turning left on Houston Street. Our last stop is:

13. **Russ and Daughters,** 179 East Houston St. (☎ 212/ 475-4880). Joel and Bella Russ began selling food from a pushcart in 1911. Their operation evolved into one of New York's most famous appetizer stores, today run by their grandson Mark Federman. At this final stop on our tour, you can stock up on Nova, creamed or schmaltz herring, whitefish salad, gefilte fish, halvah, and other Jewish delicacies, thereby taking a little of the Lower East Side home with you.

Winding Down **Katz's Delicatessen,** 205 East Houston St., at Ludlow Street (☎ 212/254-2246), is a classic New York deli that's been in business at this location since 1889. The interior is little changed from those days. Even the World War II sign reading "Send a salami to your boy in the Army" is still intact. Katz's was the setting for Meg Ryan's famous faked-orgasm scene in the movie *When Harry Met Sally.*

"She didn't really fake it," says owner Fred Austin, "it was the food." Between takes, co-star Billy Crystal, a great Katz's fan, wolfed down the equivalent of a dozen corned beef sandwiches, supplemented with hot dogs, cherry peppers, and pickles. Note the photographs of Katz's in the old days and its famous patrons hanging in the window and on the blond wood walls—everyone from Jackie Mason to Houdini to Bill Clinton. Order up a pastrami or corned beef sandwich on rye (it's stuffed with about ¾ pound of meat), a potato knish, and a New York egg cream. Austin took over the place from the Katz family about a decade ago, but hasn't changed a thing—even the archetypal surly Jewish waiter service. "If anyone's nice to a customer, I want to hear about it," he says. There's cafeteria and waiter service. Open Sunday to Wednesday 8am to 10pm, Thursday 8am to 11pm, Friday and Saturday 8am to midnight.

SoHo

Start: Broadway and Prince Street.

Subway: Take the N or R train to Prince Street.

Finish: West Broadway, just below Spring Street.

Time: Anywhere from 3 to 5 hours, depending on how long you spend browsing galleries, museums, and shops.

Best Time: Start around 10:30am, since most galleries are open 11am to 5pm (and since the breakfast stop is one of the best in the city). Return in the evening, if there are any openings, to experience the art scene at its schmooziest.

Worst Time: Sunday and Monday, when almost all galleries and most museums are closed; mid-July to early September, when many galleries are closed or open only by appointment.

Everyone has a different image that springs to mind when they hear the name New York. *Seinfeld* fans picture the Upper West Side, corporate-types imagine hitting it big on Wall Street, literary aficionados and ex-hippies have Greenwich Village flashbacks, and latter-day bohemians conjure up the East Village. Growing up with a painter for a father, my frequent trips to New York focused on one neighborhood alone, the multihued nucleus of the international art world, so a former Midtown office job and Brooklyn apartment notwithstanding, my eternal image of the Big Apple is SoHo.

Traditional SoHo—incorporating the area **so**uth of **Hous**-ton Street and north of Canal Street, bounded by Broadway and West Broadway—is roughly 1 square mile. Broadway and West Broadway run north and south with Houston Street on the north-ern tip and Canal bounding it on the south. In the early 19th century, it was a run-down zone lost between lower Manhattan and the monied mansions of uptown. Dry-goods merchant princes and emerging manufacturing companies moved in and filled the area with warehouses that incorporated the latest in cost-cutting building technology—prefabricated facades of cast iron, which represented a simple and cheap way to garnish a structure with a face that was ornate, costly looking, and stylish (which at first meant classically inspired Italian Renaissance, and later, French architectural styles). Cast-iron facades were mass produced in sections, and you could order one to fit your build-ing from a catalog and quickly assemble and bolt it to a building's frame. You could paint it any color you wished, move it to a new building if need be, and even recycle it by melting it down and recasting it when new tastes in architecture arose. The light frames made heavy outer walls unnecessary, and allowed the builders to fill up the street frontage with large windows instead. By 1962, the partially abandoned neighborhood was going to be razed to put in a highway, but architecture buffs and residents fought back, and by 1973, SoHo was declared by the city to be a his-toric district.

In the 1950s and '60s, artists, who were attracted by the low costs and huge, light-filled spaces, began renting unused floors of these warehouses (illegally, since the area wasn't zoned residential), and setting up studios with a bed in the corner for sleeping. By the 1970s, zoning restrictions had changed and more artists flooded the area. With so much art being produced, it was only natural that new art dealers, in a profession that for-merly looked only to the posh neighborhoods of Uptown, began to open up shop in SoHo. These dealers championed the neighborhood's emergent stars while turning a nice profit at the same time. Established galleries from uptown soon followed suit, and SoHo became the mecca of the contemporary art world in the late '70s and early '80s. Thrift stores and funky boutiques opened, abandoned shop fronts were filled with inexpensive din-ers, and, inevitably, the yuppies soon caught wind of it all.

In the 1980s, young professionals living in Manhattan's cramped, expensive apartments and co-ops saw the chance both to be hip and to get a huge pad at low cost by moving into converted SoHo lofts. They swarmed the neighborhood, with pricey boutiques trailing along behind. Sandwich shops like Dean and Deluca were transformed into fine food emporia. These new arrivals quickly drove the rents to the stratosphere. These trend bandwagoneers were almost universally resented by SoHo's artist community, even if some did buy the art as an investment for their empty wall space. It wasn't long before artists, even those of the nonstarving persuasion, couldn't afford to move in, and others long established in SoHo found their own rents escalating. Tourists quickly followed in the yuppies' wake, and chain stores and other paeans to mass tourism started popping up.

In the 1990s, SoHo is a neighborhood with a split personality. An artistic and pioneeringly hip air remains despite overexposure. Plenty of struggling artists' co-op exhibition spaces, funky shops, and cheap cafes still fill the streets; some galleries, like Holly Solomon, that had previously left the neighborhood for uptown have returned to their SoHo roots; and many artists continue to create in their converted apartment/studios behind historic cast-iron facades. But the hype has changed SoHo forever, from heavily commercial fine art galleries and chillingly expensive high fashion boutiques, to over-priced bistros and those yuppie-infested converted lofts. Still, there's no neighborhood quite like it, and, to me at least, none that so fully evokes the vibrancy, diversity, and creative energy that characterizes New York. Our walk through SoHo takes you past the weird industrial beauty of the cast-iron age, into some of the more interesting shops and fashion outlets, and past the doors of dozens of galleries that together provide a collective museum nonpareil of the best the international contemporary art world has to offer.

• • • • • • • • • • • • • • • •

Starting Out **Dean and Deluca,** at the southeast corner of Broadway and Prince Street, is a true New York institution. Although now expanded to multiple branches, priced a bit out of starving-artist range, and visited by as many tourists as New Yorkers, this remains one of Manhattan's older and more beloved fine food shops. It started as a lunch counter serving superb sandwiches, which you can still get inside along with a cornucopia of imported, farm-fresh, and gourmet foods, and, in the back, kitchen-ware.

SoHo

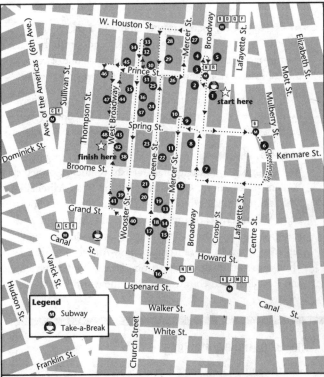

1. Lennon, Weinberg/Elga Wimmer/Cavin-Morris
2. Singer Building/Kate's Paperie
3. Guggenheim Museum SoHo
4. New Museum of Contemporary Art/
   Museum for African Art
5. The Alternative Museum/
   American Primitive Gallery
6. Eileen's Special Cheesecake
7. Haughwout Building
8. St. Nicholas Hotel
9. 101 Spring Street
10. 105 Mercer Street
11. The Enchanted Forest
12. Gourmet Garage
13. Sean Kelly
14. Yohji Yamamoto
15. Roland Feldman Fine Arts
16. Pearl Paint
17. Greene Street
18. 91-93 Grand Street/C.R.G. Gallery
19. Artists Space
20. David Zwirner/Jack Tilton Gallery
21. Gunther Building
22. "King of Greene Street"
23. agnes b. homme
24. Jekyll & Hyde/Zona
25. Richard Haas Mural
26. Miu Miu/Fanelli's Cafe
27. Holly Solomon Gallery
28. Moss
29. PaceWildenstein/Sperone Westwater/
    Phyllis Kind
30. The Metropolitan Museum of Art Shop/
    agnes b.
31. Harriet Love
32. Gagosian Gallery
33. Ricco/Maresca Gallery
34. The DIA Center/Todd Oldham/
    Bowery Gallery
35. Tony Shafrazi
36. Howard Greenberg Gallery/
    Commes des Garçons
37. Cynthia Rowley/c. i. t. e.
38. Brooke Alexander Projects
39. The Drawing Center
40. American Fine Arts, Co.
41. SoHo Books
42. Anthropologie/O. K. Harris
43. "The Broken Kilometer"
44. Nancy Hoffman
45. Louis K. Meisel Gallery
46. Vesuvio Bakery
47. Leo Castelli/Sonnabend Gallery
48. Robert Lee Morris

At the very least, grab a cappuccino and a pastry (or my favorite, a giant spiced ginger cookie) and sit at the bar counter facing the plate glass window to watch one of SoHo's busiest intersections and gird yourself for the gallery scene.

Dean and Deluca's storefront is under 560 Broadway, home to several galleries (the entrance is a few doors south on Broadway), including:

1. **Lennon, Weinberg,** on the third floor, representing many well-established contemporary artists (Chuck Connelly, Willem de Kooning, Catherine Murphy, Joan Mitchell), with leanings toward the abstract. Also on the third floor is **Elga Wimmer,** featuring contemporary American and European art. On the fourth floor is **Cavin-Morris,** showing mainly works by self-taught, non-American artists— often museum-quality works from Africa, the Caribbean, and less-developed countries around the world.

The Art of Gallery Hopping

Even to the initiated, the art world and its gallery scene can seem intimidating. But don't sweat it—treat gallery hopping more like a visit to the candy store—give an easygoing once-over to everything on display, then choose to savor the few that appeal to you the most.

Storefront galleries are the most visible, but the majority of galleries hide on the upper floors of nondescript buildings, often half a dozen or more per address. Most are open to the public unless they're hanging a new show, from 10 or 11am to 5 or 6pm Tuesday to Saturday. Mid- or late July to early September is the worst time to try to explore these galleries, as many of them shut down around this time.

Galleries present their works in the form of 4- to 6-week-long shows—either solo shows of a single artist, or a group show featuring the work of several. The lifeblood of galleries is actually selling a few of the pieces, but they know that the lion's share of people who pop by are just perusing the art, so don't feel shy about sauntering in. Also, don't feel the need to spend more time than you feel is necessary; galleries are accustomed to people who literally just poke their heads in, take a quick glance around, and withdraw quickly. You might walk through ten before you find one show that appeals to you.

If you want a brief tour of some of SoHo's founding galleries, those which have shaped the international art world since the 1950s and '60s and that still show the biggest blue-chip contemporary artists, be sure to hit Lennon, Weinberg (Stop 1), Holly Solomon (Stop 27), Pace Wildenstein and Sperone Westwater (both at Stop 29), Gagosian (Stop 32), O.K. Harris (Stop 42), Nancy Hoffman (Stop 44), and Leo Castelli and Sonnabend (both at Stop 47). For Photography, check out Howard Greenberg (Stop 36). For nontraditional and nonwestern art, try Cavin-Morris (Stop 1), the American Primitive Gallery (Stop 5) and the Museum for African Art (Stop 4).

Although you should take this walking tour during the day, the best way to catch a glimpse into the living New York art world is to attend the evening "opening" of a new show, most of which are open to the public. *The Village Voice* newspaper, the "Weekend" section of Friday's *New York Times,* and *The New Yorker* and *New York* magazines all list upcoming openings, as well as current shows. For even more complete information, pick up a free copy of *The Gallery Guide* at just about any museum or gallery.

As you exit 560 Broadway, you'll see across the street the terra-cotta facade and long, graceful arches of the:

2. **Singer Building,** designed by Ernest Flagg in 1904 as an office and warehouse for the sewing machine giant. The 12-story facade with large glass windows and a steel frame was an architectural novelty at the time, and prefigured the plate-glass walls of later 20th-century skyscrapers.

The Singer building's ground floor is taken up with **Kate's Paperie** (☎ 212/633-0570), selling paper and stationery items of the highest quality and inventiveness, along with housewares in the back. Cross Broadway to at least poke your head in for a glance at the paper geometry of the ceiling. Then cross Prince Street so you're standing on the northwest corner at the start of SoHo's museum row. Filling the russet 19th-century building at this corner is the:

3. **Guggenheim Museum SoHo** (☎ 212/423-3500), a branch of New York's modern art museum. SoHo's Guggenheim curates many single-artist shows and is a bit more contemporary than the more famous Guggenheim uptown. Recent highlighted artists have included Jeff Koons and architects Arakawa and Madeline Gins. You don't have to pay admission to browse the outstanding museum shop. Hours are Sunday and Tuesday to Friday 11am to 6pm, Saturday 11am to 8pm.

A few doors up Broadway at no. 583 is:

4. **The New Museum of Contemporary Art** (☎ 212/219-1222). In 1977, Marcia Tucker left her post as curator of the Whitney Museum on ideological grounds. The Whitney, as most museums, showcased mainly works of establishment-approved artists who were either dead or past the vital, relevant stage of their careers. Tucker founded this New Museum with no permanent collection, devoted rather to the works of significant contemporary artists who have helped shape the world's current art scene. Through group and solo exhibitions, the museum displays works by a wide range of international painters, photographers, and sculptors. It's hours are Wednesday to Friday and Sunday noon to 6pm, Saturday noon to 8pm.

For a very different sort of art, walk another few doors up Broadway to no. 593 and **The Museum for African Art** (☎ 212/966-1313). The collections here are particularly rich, with ever-changing exhibits showcasing the history and diversity of Africa's art forms, from the prehistoric to the contemporary. As with the Guggenheim, even if you don't plan to pay admission to visit the museum, the book/gift shop is definitely worth stopping in for. Hours are Tuesday to Friday 10:30am to 5:30pm, Saturday and Sunday noon to 6pm.

Across Broadway at no. 594 is:

5. **The Alternative Museum** (☎ 212/966-4444), located on the fourth floor of no. 594. Another museum devoted

to the living, working artist, the Alternative tends to focus on cutting edge, hot-ticket names who explore the emergent technological sides of art and image—video, computers, electronic installations. Hours are Tuesday to Saturday 11am to 6pm.

Also in this building, on the second floor, is the **American Primitive Gallery,** displaying a range of works produced by so-called naive or primitive artists—ones who are self-taught. Often with strong, simple messages or a touch of whimsy, this art can be a refreshing antidote to the often overthought and overwrought works in other SoHo galleries by more formally trained artists.

Turn south down Broadway, passing back by Dean and Deluca, to Spring Street and turn left. You're now heading out of traditional SoHo, into the remnants of Little Italy. But this area bounded by Lafayette and Elizabeth streets is a hipper, newer, happening scene, more sophisticated, and much less touristy than SoHo. It has a European flair, a few modest galleries, and lots of good small restaurants and bistros.

Take a Break At 80 Spring St. at the corner of Crosby, **Balthazar** (☎ **212/965-1414**) is a trendy spot that faithfully replicates a large Parisian bistro, with high pressed-tin ceilings, lazily turning fans, and animated conversation rising from closely pressed tables—talk that is as likely to cover the European Union and the New York art scene as well as the latest Wall Street trend or Madonna video (the pop diva herself has been known to nosh here). Hors d'oeuvres include a velvety warm goat cheese and caramelized onion tart, and spinach and arugula ravioli. The grilled brook trout or chicken paillard salad are equally mouth-watering, and with entrees ranging from roasted salmon to bouillabaisse (Fridays) to plain old hamburger with pommes frites, there's something for everyone. Main dishes run $9.50 to $21; save room for dessert at the next stop. Balthazar is open daily noon to 2am (Friday and Saturday until 3am), with Saturday and Sunday brunch served 11:30am to 4pm. There's an attached boulangerie bread shop if you just want to grab a quick bite.

Continue east on Spring Street to animated Lafayette Street, home to funky antique shops (lots of retro '50s and

'60s stuff), cafes, and pop art's first officially sanctioned outlet store, Keith Haring's Pop Shop (off this tour, a few blocks north at no. 292). If you look to your right, you'll see that Lafayette Street forks half a block down. Cross over Lafayette here at Spring Street to walk down the east side of Lafayette, so that you can take the left-hand branch of the fork, called Cleveland Place. Another half a block down, at 17 Cleveland Place and the corner of Kenmare Street is the tiny:

6. **Eileen's Special Cheesecake** (☎ 212/966-5585). Eileen Avezzano started making cheesecakes in her kitchen for neighbors in the early '70s; now she FedExes them all over the United States. Cupped in hand-molded graham cracker crusts, these little pies are held by many (clients include Robert Redford, Peter Falk, and Frank Sinatra) to be the best cheesecakes in New York. Two dollars will get you a minicheesecake in any of about 19 variations, from plain to fruit-topped to chocolate-and-raspberry swirl.

Continue on the short block down Cleveland Place to Broome Street and turn right. At the corner of Broadway, you'll see on your right the flank of the:

7. **Haughwout Building.** This cast-iron building was built in 1857 for E.V. Haughwout china and glassware company, one-time supplier to the White House. It is a perfect example of how the cast-iron movement was a phenomenon where aesthetic sensibilities of past eras (in this case Renaissance Italy) met with the practicality and technical skill and replication perfection of the industrial age. The architect used a single element (a window arch) from Jacopo Sansavino's Renaissance Biblioteca on Venice's St. Mark's Square and based this entire cast-iron facade upon it, taking what was once merely a single part of a complex Renaissance structure and repeating it 92 times to make a new, industrial whole. This was also the first building to use the steam-driven Otis safety elevator, a contraption that freed buildings from limiting their height to a comfortable walk-up and allowed skyscrapers to soar.

Turn right up Broadway to admire the front of the Haughwout as you head back north. As you near Spring Street, look across Broadway to see the bits of marble facade that remain from the:

8. **St. Nicholas Hotel** (nos. 521–23). This luxury hotel from the 1850s cost more than $1 million to build—with its velvet pile carpets, silk chair covers, and embroidered mosquito nettings—but reaped even greater profits during the heyday of downtown high society. The Civil War spelled the end of its glory days (in fact, it served time as the area's Union Army headquarters) and by the 1870s when the glitterati scene moved uptown, it had closed for good.

    Swing left on Spring Street. At the corner of Mercer Street is:

9. **101 Spring St.,** an 1870 cast-iron masterpiece with huge windows that architecturally looked forward to the age of skyscrapers.

    Turn right onto Mercer Street a few steps and look across the street at one of the oldest houses surviving in SoHo, built in 1831:

10. **105 Mercer St.,** which by 1832 was already doing brisk business as a brothel. In the mid-19th century, what is now called SoHo was New York's largest, and most genteel, red light district. Mercer Street was lined with houses of illicit pleasure, and a full two-thirds of Gotham's ladies of the night trolled the streets looking for likely clients and plied their prostrate trade in rooms on the upper floors of buildings like this one. By the end of the Civil War, the cream of the prostitute crop had moved uptown (arm-in-arm with high society), and SoHo's bordellos declined into true houses of ill repute, fit only for drunken sailors.

    Manhattan businesses began razing these old buildings to put up warehouses on the cheap property, and the cast-iron age was born. This wooden house is one of Manhattan's oldest former brothels still standing (now a private home).

    Turn around to walk south down Mercer Street. In the next block on the right is:

11. **The Enchanted Forest** (☎ 212/925-6677) at no. 85, a boutique hawking handmade and other innovative children's toys, books, and stuffed animals in a setting evoking rain forest–meets–fairy tale.

    Continue south to Broome Street, where at the far corner, you'll see the:

12. **Gourmet Garage** (☎ 212/941-5850), a specialty foods and sandwich shop similar to Dean and Deluca, but more oriented toward organic, rather than imported, fine foods.

    A block farther down Mercer Street on the left, just before Grand Street, is the gallery of:

13. **Sean Kelly,** which shows contemporary art with an emphasis on conceptual projects (Thomas Joshua Cooper, Ann Hamilton, Joseph Kosuth, Lorna Simpson).

    At the southwest corner of Mercer and Grand, at no. 103 Grand St., is the chillingly expensive:

14. **Yohji Yamamoto** (☎ 212/966-9066), a Japanese designer clothing boutique with elegantly stylish wares. The fashion here is overwhelmingly basic black, but the Mondrian-print raincoat does make an occasional appearance on the racks.

    Continue down Mercer to no. 31 and:

15. **Roland Feldman Fine Arts.** This is a gallery of the very avant-garde, with several shows a year showcasing the designs of some of the most interesting architects working in America (Arakawa, Joseph Beuys, Leon Golub).

    Trek down the last stretch of Mercer to Canal Street, across which you'll see the unmistakable, dingy white-and-red edifice of:

16. **Pearl Paint** (☎ 212/431-7932) at 308 Canal, quite possibly the world's greatest art supply store. It's certainly one of the largest, offering more than 45,000 items on six floors, all at a discount. There's an artist in all of us, and the mazelike tunnels of Pearl's narrow aisles piled high with the raw materials of creativity are fun to explore.

    Cross back to the north side of busy Canal and walk one block west to:

17. **Greene Street,** with the highest concentration of cast-iron facades in the world—50 buildings in these five SoHo blocks. The first block alone, between Canal and Grand, has on the right (east) side a full 13 (from no. 8 to 34), the longest continuous row left anywhere. Across the street, nos. 15–17 is a late example (1895) done in simple, Corinthian style. Back on the right, nos. 28–30 is known as the **"Queen of Greene Street,"** perhaps the finest cast-iron building ever erected. Is was designed in 1872 by master Isaac F.

Duckworth when French tastes had superseded the original Italian. Hence, this is a Second Empire–style facade with a mansard roof.

At Grand Street, detour right to see:

18. **91–93 Grand St.,** one of the most successfully illusory cast-iron facades. The frontage is made up of iron plates bolted together so seamlessly that the building appears to be made of cut stone blocks. In the storefront of no. 93 is the contemporary **C.R.G. Gallery.**

Turn right back up Greene Street, and immediately on your right, at third floor of no. 38, is:

19. **Artists Space,** which curates exhibits of young, undiscovered artists, before they get embroiled in the capriciously trendy feeding frenzy of the gallery scene.

Across the street and a bit farther north (no. 43) is the contemporary gallery of:

20. **David Zwirner,** who puts on quality solo exhibitions (Hans Accola, Douglas Kolk), often with a conceptual slant. His neighbor at no. 49 is the **Jack Tilton Gallery,** showing contemporary painting and sculpture, both by individual artists (David Sher, Nancy Spero, Fred Tomaselli) and by theme ("New China," of contemporary Chinese artists, was up in the summer of 1997).

Continue north on Greene Street. As you cross Broome, look back over your left shoulder to see the elaborate:

21. **Gunther Building,** with its curved corner windows on the southwest corner of Broome and Greene streets.

A short way up the next block on your right (nos. 72–76) rises the:

22. **"King of Greene Street,"** another cast-iron masterpiece designed by that genius of the genre, Isaac Duckworth. The ornate and complex classical facade makes liberal use of Corinthian columns and decorative detail.

Across the street, at no. 79, is:

23. **agnes b. homme** (☎ 212/431-4339), SoHo's men's outlet of the famed French designer.

If agnes b. doesn't catch your fancy, continue north on Greene Street, past Spring Street, to no. 93 and:

24. **Jekyll and Hyde** (☎ 212/966-8503), another menswear boutique, featuring British and European labels so hot they won't be "in" until next month.

   Next door, at no. 97, is **Zona** (☎ 212/925-6750), a furniture and housewares store with a serious American West/Southwest slant tinged with a bit of south of the border (they also serve good blended fruit smoothies if your energy is flagging).

   At Prince Street, cross to the right (east) side of the street, turn around, and look back across Greene to see the:

25. **Richard Haas Mural.** If cast-iron facades were originally conceived of as illusory imitations of more expensive stone facades, then Richard Haas's trompe l'oeil mural—a painted facsimile of a cast-iron facade—is quite the bit of irony (no pun intended). Look for the contented cat sitting in a half-open window that helps complete the illusion.

   Turn right and walk down Prince Street. On your right you'll find:

26. **Miu Miu** (☎ 212/334-5156), a women's wear division of Prada. The racks usually hides at least a few affordable pieces of the firm's elegant designer clothing. Continue east on Prince Street. At the corner of Mercer Street stands an old Manhattan holdover, **Fanelli's Cafe** (☎ 226-9412). Established in 1847, this is the second oldest bar in New York, named Fanelli's in 1922 (when it was operating as a speakeasy). Within the turn-of-the-century interior, a clientele of surprisingly regular-looking folk (not wacky *artiste* types) roam about.

   After a refreshing mug of ale (and perhaps a bracing cup of soup from the sidewalk kiosk just around the corner on the Mercer Street side of Fanelli's), turn left up Mercer Street to the corner of Houston Street and the:

27. **Holly Solomon Gallery.** Ms. Solomon was one of the very first SoHo dealers, opening shop in 1969, and after a sojourn on Fifth Avenue is back in the neighborhood. Her huge, multilevel space allows for shows of three or four contemporary artists, often leaning to the avant-garde and mixed-media, as well as photography and installations. Featured artists include Jeff Perrone, Kim MacConnel, William Wegman, and Nam June Paik.

Turn left onto Houston Street and left again back onto Greene Street. Immediately on your left, at no. 146, is:

28. **Moss** (☎ 212/226-8473), a homewares design shack of exquisite taste, representing the best and most expensive of 20th-century design. It's something between a museum and a shop, showcasing everything that's hot, from the rubber vases of Holland's Droog Design and flexible plastic bookshelves that undulate along the wall, to inventive flatware and the collective output from Italy's Alessi firm, including colorful cat-faced bottle openers, Robert Graves's whim-sical tea kettles, and phallic butane lighters.

A few doors farther down the block is 142 Greene St., home to several important galleries, including a giant:

29. **PaceWildenstein,** a front-runner in the international art world, with two New York locations exhibiting blue-chip artists of 20th-century American and European painting, drawing, and sculpture. The short list includes Georg Baselitz, Alexander Calder, Chuck Close, Jim Dine, Jean Dubuffet, Agnes Martin, Louise Nevelson, Isamu Noguchi, Claes Oldenburg, Pablo Picasso, Robert Rauschenberg, Mark Rothko, Julian Schnabel, and Richard Serra.

At the same address, with a slightly less overwhelming atmosphere, is the New York branch of the Rome-based dealer **Sperone Westwater** (second floor). Although less intimidating than PaceWildenstein, it still features high quality, big-name 20th-century artists. Some of Sperone's stars include Francesco Clemente, Bruce Naumann, Susan Rothenberg, Richard Tuttle, Cy Twombly, and William Wegman.

Farther south on Greene Street, at no. 136, lies the **Phyllis Kind Gallery,** which tends to show eccentric artists from across America—Chicagoans Roger Brown and Jim Nutt; Robert Colescott's historical, African American–themed paintings; and photographer Alison Sarr.

Continue down Greene Street to Prince and turn right (there's the Richard Haas mural again). If you need a break from the avant-garde and want to slip back into the world of pre–20th century art, pop into no. 113 on your right, a branch of:

30. **The Metropolitan Museum of Art Shop** (☎ 212/ 614-3000). Across the street, next to SoHo's bronze Goddess of Overfertility, is the women's wear boutique for French designer **agnes b.** (nos. 116–18).

    Keep heading west on Prince Street a few doors to no. 126:

31. **Harriet Love** (☎ 212/966-2280), one of the original artist-era SoHo shops, selling vintage jewelry and vintage and reproduction clothes for women.

    Turn right up Wooster Street. On your right, at no. 136—the unobtrusive entrance next to a huge garage door— is a beautifully converted space housing SoHo's branch of the:

32. **Gagosian Gallery.** This venerable gallery is somewhat traditionalist, sticking to its guns with big-name, mainly American, highly regarded male artists, an A-list that includes Francesco Clemente, Walter de Maria, Mark di Suervo, David Salle, Richard Serra, Frank Stella, and Andy Warhol. Gagosian received plenty of press when British shock artist Damien Hirst unveiled here his vats of vivisected and pickled livestock and called it art.

    A bit farther north on Wooster brings you to no. 152 and the:

33. **Ricco/Maresca Gallery,** a space where experimental artists can push the art envelope; a recent show highlighted the computer-altered images of Nancy Burson.

    Turning around to walk south back down Wooster Street, on your left at no. 141, is one of the many branches of:

34. **The DIA Center for the Arts.** Although ostensibly they occasionally change the exhibition at this art, lecture, and symposia center, Walter de Maria's terraform work "The New York Earth Room" has been filling the space immobile since 1977. (If you have the chance while in New York, by all means visit the DIA Center's headquarters in the heart of Chelsea's gallery scene at 548 West 22nd St.)

    Continuing south on Wooster, cross Prince Street and on your right at no. 123 is the **Todd Oldham Store** (☎ 212/219-3531), a boutique of designer women's clothing so trendy it's ugly. Next door at no. 121 is the **Bowery**

Gallery, yet another fine outlet for contemporary art. No. 119 is home to the well-known gallery of:

35. **Tony Shafrazi,** which still carries a torch for the 1980s Pop Art movement and the East Village Artists. Recent shows have spotlighted Jean-Michel Basquiat, Keith Haring, Julian Schnabel, Donald Baechler, and Kenny Scharf.

    Across the street and a few steps back up Wooster is the:

36. **Howard Greenberg Gallery,** on the second floor of no. 120, a dignified and well-endowed gallery devoted to classic (and some contemporary) 20th-century photography. They represent exclusively Imogen Cunningham and Marc Riboud, and have an impressive catalogue of artists including Bernice Abbott, Margaret Bourke-White, Dorothea Lange, Jacob Riis, Edward Steichen, and Alfred Steiglitz.

    Continue down Wooster Street and do some window shopping at no. 116, **Comme des Garçons** (☎ 212/219-0660). Japanese designer Rei Kawakuba's monochrome, sculptural clothing has been a fashion staple since 1981. This is a new showroom, but the boutique has long been one of the main suppliers to the gallery show-opening set.

    A bit farther down the block at no. 112 is the boutique of:

37. **Cynthia Rowley** (☎ 212/334-1144), a young designer of women's fashions. Her neighbor at 104 Wooster is the studio (sorry, no boutique here) of fashion darling **Isaac Mizrahi,** who seems to be able to work a clothing line based on any theme (the last few years saw him inspired first by insects, then by street bums).

    Near the corner of Spring Street (no. 100) is the funky little **c.i.t.e.** (☎ 212/431-7272), an antique shop of 1950s-era furniture and housewares, for the kitschy or just plain nostalgic.

    You have a block of breathing space continuing south on Wooster until just before you reach Broome Street, where on the right, on the second floor of no. 59, is:

38. **Brooke Alexander Projects,** one of the most important contemporary print galleries in New York. Along with the occasional installation, the American and European artists shown here tend to be well established: Joseph Albers,

Georg Baselitz, Lucien Freud, Jasper Johns, Donald Judd, Robert Mangold, Bruce Nauman, Claes Oldenburg, and Robert Rauschenberg, among others.

Keep walking south on Wooster Street. In the next block, at no. 35, is:

39. **The Drawing Center,** a prestigious not-for-profit outfit that since 1976 has been instrumental in getting emerging and under-represented artists' work some SoHo air-time. There are usually three annual experimental shows of new artists, and one (held April to July) of museum-quality historic drawings (1997 pickings included the likes of Rembrandt, Guercino, and architects Gaudi and Inigo Jones). Across the street at no. 40, they've opened up "The Drawing Room," for even more experimental projects and installations.

Keep walking south, just past Grand Street on the left (no. 22 Wooster) is the:

40. **American Fine Arts, Co.,** specializing in conceptual contemporary art. Every spring, they put on a show of the "Art Club 2000," a group of artists (mainly photographers) formed at Cooper Union.

Return up Wooster Street to Grand Street and then from there, take a left. At West Broadway, take a right to walk up the east (closest) side. Start with a bookworm's dream:

41. **SoHo Books** (☎ 212/226-3395), an emporium of heavily discounted books, both new (usually overrun and unsold hardback editions) and used. Out front, the spanking new books on tables usually go for around $1.98.

☕ **Take a Break** The **Cupping Room Cafe** (☎ 212/925-2898) at 359 Broadway has an eclectic menu, eclectic atmosphere (with some intimate corners), and a good selection of wines by the glass. On the $14 to $22 side of the menu, recommendable entrees range from pork chops with apple chutney to grilled mahimahi with tomato coulis. The sandwich half of the menu is somewhat more reasonable, running around $7 to $12 for the like of burgers and fries, or black forest ham with Jarlsberg on pumpernickel. For dessert, the unique white hot chocolate goes well with any of the to-die-for fresh cakes and pastries, which are all made on the premises.

Continue north up West Broadway. Half a block past Broome, at no. 375, you'll find:

42. **Anthropologie,** a mix of clothing, homewares, and odd sundries that evokes a warehouse-sized version of a Banana Republic store, but with a vaguely Dr.-Livingstone-I-presume tone.

At no. 383 Broadway is **O.K. Harris,** another of the surviving '70s galleries in SoHo, with the distinction of showcasing large quantities of American art in a variety of styles and artists. Some are attracted to its multiple large showrooms and seemingly inexhaustible supply of works to suit any taste, others scorn it as a "supermarket of art."

Meandering farther up West Broadway, at no. 393 is a second SoHo DIA Center, this one showcasing:

43. **"The Broken Kilometer,"** another semipermanent installation by Walter de Maria. One kilometer's worth of steel cylinder segments lie end to end in the room here; legend has it that another set of cylinders are arranged sticking out of the ground to make a grid, one kilometer square, out in a remote desert area of the American Southwest. This desert has an abnormally high frequency of lightning, and the steel cylinders act as lightning rods, causing the electricity to play about the grid.

Keep heading north on West Broadway. Halfway up the next block (no. 429) is the gallery of:

44. **Nancy Hoffman,** a real '70s gallery, both in its style and its artists, that has managed to remain virtually unchanged since the day it opened and SoHo was just coming into its own as a gallery scene. Perhaps the last of its breed, Nancy Hoffman is not considered the cutting edge anymore, but it's still a quality gallery.

Continue up West Broadway to Prince Street and detour right to no. 141 Prince St., the:

45. **Louis K. Meisel Gallery,** a major exhibition space for photorealists like John Clem Clark, Chuck Close, Richard Estes, Mel Ramos, and Edward Runci.

Return to West Broadway, cross it, and continue down Prince Street to no. 160 on the left, the:

46. **Vesuvio Bakery,** a real old-fashioned Italian bakery that's been in the Dapolito family since 1920. The green-edged

plate windows are usually stacked high with a balancing act of breads leaned straight up against it, with a few ring-shaped loafs perched on top for effect.

Turn around and make your way back to West Broadway, taking a right to head south back down the west side of the street. On your right, at no. 420, you will find two of the biggest names in the art world, starting on the second floor with:

47. **Leo Castelli.** He was the single most important dealer in America in the late 1950s through the '60s. Castelli discovered or helped make famous many of the artists that now hold pride of place in modern art museums—Claes Oldenberg, Donald Judd, Jasper Johns, Frank Stella, Roy Lichtenstein, Richard Serra, Robert Morris, Keith Sonnier, and Bruce Nauman, among others. Castelli was also one of the first galleries to open a space in SoHo, around 1970. Although it's no longer as relevant to the art scene, as of 1997 the nonagenarian Castelli was still running his showrooms in the tradition that made him a major force in the art world.

Also in this building, on the third floor, is another big international name, the **Sonnabend Gallery.** More avantgarde than its neighbor, Sonnabend shows contemporary American and European art, with big-ticket names that include minimalist Mel Bochner, Carroll Dunham, the team of Gilbert and George with their larger-than-life photographs walking the tightrope of good taste, photographers Anne and Patrick Poirier, Robert Rauschenberg, and Terry Winters (major force in the '80s painting scene).

You just have one last leg left; walk south on West Broadway, just past Spring Street, and the official SoHo tour ends at no. 400:

48. **Robert Lee Morris,** the studio and showroom of this hot jewelry designer.

☕ **Winding Down** If you still have the energy to walk 2½ blocks down the rest of West Broadway to just before Canal Street, you can climb to the second floor of the modern **SoHo Grand Hotel,** take a seat at the fashionable and well-designed bar (where many postopening crowds gather), and toast the glory days of SoHo's art world.

Greenwich Village Literary Tour

Start: Bleecker Street between La Guardia Place and Thompson Street.

Subway: Take the 6 to Bleecker Street, which lets you out at Bleecker and Lafayette streets. Walk west on Bleecker.

Finish: 14 West 10th St.

Time: Approximately 4 to 5 hours.

Best Time: If you plan to do the whole tour, start fairly early in the day (there's a breakfast break near the start).

The Village has always attracted rebels, radicals, and creative types—from earnest 18th-century revolutionary Thomas Paine, to early 20th-century radicals such as John Reed and Mabel Dodge, to the Stonewall rioters who gave birth to the gay liberation movement in 1969. It was even a Village protest in 1817 that saved the area's colorfully

Greenwich Village Literary Tour

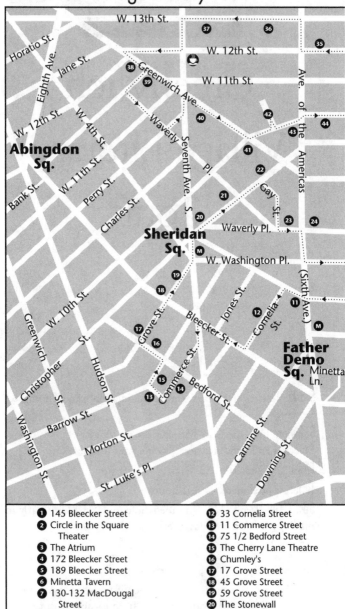

1. 145 Bleecker Street
2. Circle in the Square Theater
3. The Atrium
4. 172 Bleecker Street
5. 189 Bleecker Street
6. Minetta Tavern
7. 130-132 MacDougal Street
8. 85 West 3rd Street
9. The Provincetown Playhouse
10. 137 MacDougal Street
11. Sixth Avenue and West 4th Street
12. 33 Cornelia Street
13. 11 Commerce Street
14. 75 1/2 Bedford Street
15. The Cherry Lane Theatre
16. Chumley's
17. 17 Grove Street
18. 45 Grove Street
19. 59 Grove Street
20. The Stonewall
21. Waverly Place & Christopher Street
22. Gay Street
23. 139 Waverly Place
24. 116 Waverly Place

7-0019

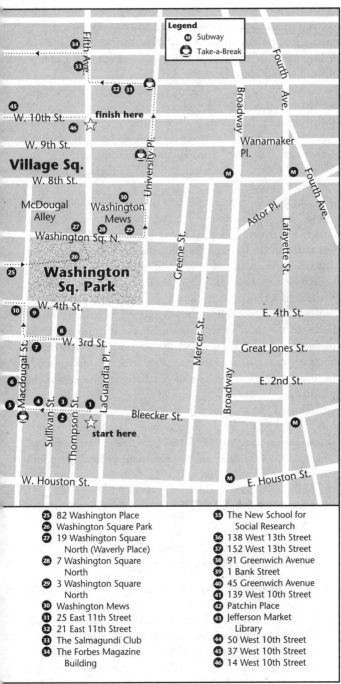

25 82 Washington Place
26 Washington Square Park
27 19 Washington Square North (Waverly Place)
28 7 Washington Square North
29 3 Washington Square North
30 Washington Mews
31 25 East 11th Street
32 21 East 11th Street
33 The Salmagundi Club
34 The Forbes Magazine Building
35 The New School for Social Research
36 138 West 13th Street
37 152 West 13th Street
38 91 Greenwich Avenue
39 1 Bank Street
40 45 Greenwich Avenue
41 139 West 10th Street
42 Patchin Place
43 Jefferson Market Library
44 50 West 10th Street
45 37 West 10th Street
46 14 West 10th Street

convoluted lanes and byways when the city imposed a geo-
metric grid system on the rest of New York streets. Much of
Village life centers around Washington Square Park, site of hippie rallies and counterculture demonstrations, as well as the
former stomping ground of Henry James and Edith Wharton.

Many other American writers have, at some time, made
their homes in the Village. As early as the 19th century it was
New York's literary hub—venue for salons and other intellectual
gatherings. Both the Metropolitan Museum of Art and the
Whitney Museum of American Art came into being here, albeit
some 60 years apart.

The 20th century saw this area transformed from a bastion
of old New York families to a bohemian enclave of struggling
writers and artists. Though skyrocketing rents made the Village
less accessible to aspiring artists after the late 1920s, it remained
a mecca for creative people—so much so that almost every building is a literary landmark. Today, the sheer cost of housing here
has seen to it that most modern Villagers are upwardly mobile
professionals. There still are, however, plenty of resident throw-
backs to the '60s, latter-day bohemians of multiple body
piercings, earnest NYU students, gawking tourists, funky shops,
and great cafes that keep this one of the liveliest neighborhoods
in town. And it remains one of Manhattan's most downright
picturesque corners.

Though the focus of this tour is the Village's literary history, I think you'll also enjoy strolling along its quaint, tree-
shaded streets lined with Federal and Greek revival buildings.
This tour is a long one, and you may want to break it up into
two visits.

• • • • • • • • • • • • • • • • •

Begin on Bleecker Street, named for a writer, Anthony
Bleecker, whose friends included Washington Irving and
William Cullen Bryant, at:

1. **145 Bleecker St.,** where James Fenimore Cooper,
   author of 32 novels, plus a dozen works of nonfiction, lived
   in 1833. Though he is primarily remembered for romantic
   adventure stories of American frontier, Cooper also wrote
   political commentary, naval history, sea stories, and a group
   of novels about the Middle Ages. His father—judge,

congressman, and Federalist Party leader William Cooper—founded Cooperstown, New York, the author's childhood home. This was the setting for the author's *Leatherstocking Tales,* the epic of the frontiersman Natty Bumppo (written over a period of 19 years), which includes *The Pioneers, The Last of the Mohicans, The Prairie, The Pathfinder,* and *The Deerslayer.* The town is certainly more famous today as the home of the Baseball Hall of Fame.

James F. Cooper entered Yale at age 13 (not an uncommon occurrence in the early 19th century) but was expelled in his junior year for pranks like putting a donkey in a professor's chair. At 17, his aborted college career was followed by a stint in the merchant marines and the navy. His first novel, *Precaution,* was published in 1820. It created no great stir in the literary world, but a second novel focusing on the American Revolution, *The Spy*, appeared a year later and enjoyed vast success, as did his later books.

Continue west (walk right) to:

2. **Circle in the Square Theater,** 159 Bleecker St., founded by Ted Mann and Jose Quintero in 1951 at the site of an abandoned nightclub on Sheridan Square; it moved to Bleecker Street in 1959. It was one of the first arena, or "in-the-round," theaters in the United States. Tennessee Williams's *Summer and Smoke* (starring Geraldine Page), Eugene O'Neill's *The Iceman Cometh* (starring Jason Robards, Jr.), Thorton Wilder's *Plays for Bleecker Street,* Truman Capote's *The Grass Harp,* and Jean Genet's *The Balcony* all premiered here. Actors Colleen Dewhurst, Dustin Hoffman, James Earl Jones, Cicely Tyson, Jason Robards, George C. Scott, and Peter Falk honed their craft on the Circle in the Square stage. And Sunday lectures and readings in the early 1950s featured Gore Vidal, Dorothy Parker, Tennessee Williams, Arthur Miller, and many other illustrious authors. The theater continues to present high-quality productions of important plays.

Across the street is:

3. **The Atrium** (no. 160), a 19th-century beaux arts building by Ernest Flagg that is today a posh apartment building. Before becoming the sadly defunct Village Gate jazz club in the late 1950s, this former flophouse was Theodore

Dreiser's first New York residence (in 1895, he paid 25¢ a night for a cell-like room).

Further west is:

4. **172 Bleecker St.,** where James Agee lived in a top floor railroad flat from 1941 to 1951, after he completed *Let Us Now Praise Famous Men*. Though the book enjoyed a great vogue in the 1960s, it was originally scathingly reviewed and went out of print in 1948 after selling a mere 1,025 copies. Ralph Thompson of *The New York Times* called Agee "arrogant, mannered, precious, gross," and his book "the choicest recent example of how to write self-inspired, self-conscious, and self-indulgent prose." *Time* called it "the most distinguished failure of the season."

Rallying from critical buffets, during his Bleecker Street tenancy, Agee created the screenplay for *The African Queen* and worked as a movie critic for both *Time* and *The Nation*. He had to move from this walk-up apartment after he suffered a heart attack.

Nearby, the quintessential Village corner of Bleecker and MacDougal, is a good spot for a breakfast break.

Take a Break Café Figaro (☎ 212/677-1100), at 184–186 Bleecker St., is an old beat-generation haunt. In 1969, Village residents were disheartened to see the Figaro close and in its place arise an uninspired and sterile Blimpie's. In 1976, the present owner completely restored Figaro to its earlier appearance, replastering its walls once again with shellacked copies of the French newspaper *Le Figaro*. Stop in for pastries and coffee or an omelet and absorb the atmosphere, or sit at a sidewalk table to watch the Village parade by. It opens at 10:30am Monday to Friday and serves a full fixed-price brunch Saturday and Sunday from 10am to 3pm.

On the opposite corner is:

5. **189 Bleecker St.** For several decades, beginning in the late 1920s, the San Remo (today Carpo's Cafe), an Italian restaurant at the corner of Bleecker and MacDougal streets, was a writer's hangout frequented by James Baldwin, William Styron, Jack Kerouac, James Agee, Frank O'Hara, Gregory Corso, Dylan Thomas, William Burroughs, and Allen Ginsberg. John Clellon Holmes wrote about the San

Remo in his 1952 novel, *Go,* one of the first published works of the beat generation.

Take a right and head north on MacDougal Street to the:

6. **Minetta Tavern,** 113 MacDougal St., at Minetta Lane (☎ 212/475-3850), which was a speakeasy called the Black Rabbit during Prohibition. The most unlikely event to take place here in those wild days was the founding of De Witt Wallace's very unbohemian *Reader's Digest* on the premises in 1923; the magazine was published in the basement in its early days. Since 1937, the Minetta has been a simpatico Italian restaurant and meeting place for writers and other creative folk, including Ezra Pound, e.e. cummings, Louis Bromfield, and Ernest Hemingway.

   The Minetta still evokes the old Village. Walls are covered with photographs of famous patrons and caricatures (about 20 of which artist Franz Kline scrawled in exchange for drinks and food), and the rustic pine-paneled back room is adorned with murals of local landmarks. Stop in for a drink or a meal. The Minetta is open daily from noon to midnight serving traditional Italian fare.

   Minetta Lane is named for the Minetta Brook that started on 23rd Street and flowed through here en route to the Hudson. The brook still runs underground.

   A little farther up and across the street stands an 1852 house fronted by twin entrances and a wisteria-covered portico.

7. **130–132 MacDougal St.** belonged to Louisa May Alcott's uncle and, after the Civil War, Alcott lived and worked here. Historians believe it was here she penned her best-known work, the autobiographical children's classic *Little Women* (Jo, Amy, Meg, and Beth were based on Alcott and her sisters Abbie, Anna, and Lizzie, respectively). Alcott grew up in Concord, Massachusetts, the daughter of transcendentalist Amos Bronson Alcott. Emerson was a close family friend, and Thoreau taught the young Louisa botany. During the Civil War, Alcott briefly served as a Union hospital nurse in Washington, D.C., (until a case of typhoid fever nearly killed her). Alcott later published a book of letters documenting that time under the title *Hospital Sketches.* Mercury poisoning from the medication left her

in fragile health the rest of her life. Henry James called Alcott "The novelist of children . . . the Thackery, the Trollope, of the nursery and schoolroom." Die-hard chauvinist G.K. Chesterton found himself admitting in 1907 that "even from a masculine standpoint, the books are very good."

Turn right onto West 3rd St. Walk one block; just beyond Sullivan Street, to:

8. **85 West 3rd St.,** Edgar Allan Poe lived, on the third floor, in 1845 (last window on the right). He wrote *Facts in the Case of M. Valdemar* here, and *The Raven* was published during his tenancy. Today, it's part of NYU Law School, and the current residents claim Poe's rooms are haunted.

Double back down 3rd Street to MacDougal Street and turn right. On your left is:

9. **The Provincetown Playhouse,** 133 MacDougal St. (☎ 212/477-5048), was first established in 1915 on a wharf in Provincetown, Massachusetts. Founders George Cram "Jig" Cook and his wife Susan Glaspell began by producing their own plays. One day, however, an intense 27-year-old named Eugene O'Neill arrived in Provincetown with a trunk full of plays, a few of which he brought for Cook and Glaspell to read. They immediately recognized his genius and were inspired to create a theater dedicated to experimental drama. It moved to this converted stable, where O'Neill managed it through 1927. Many of O'Neill's early plays premiered here—*Bound East for Cardiff, The Hairy Ape, The Long Voyage Home, The Emperor Jones,* and *All God's Chillun's Got Wings.* That last play was especially radical for its time, portraying a racially mixed couple; star Paul Robeson actually kissed white actress Mary Blair (literary critic Edmund Wilson's wife) on stage, prompting general outrage and Ku Klux Klan threats. Nevertheless, the play ran for 5 months.

Other seminal figures in the theater's early days were Max Eastman, Djuna Barnes, Edna Ferber, and John Reed. Edna St. Vincent Millay, whose unlikely life plan was to support herself as a poet by earning her living as an actress, snagged both the lead in Fred Dell's *An Angel Intrudes,* and Dell himself (their love affair inspired her poems *Weeds* and *Journal*). Millay's own work, *Aria da Capo,* was produced here in 1919. Another notable Provincetown Playhouse production was e.e. cummings's *him*, a play with 21 scenes and 105 characters.

Katharine Cornell, Tallulah Bankhead, Bette Davis (who made her stage debut here), and Eva Le Gallienne appeared on the Provincetown stage in its early years. The theater was a great success, and O'Neill's plays went on to Broadway. But instead of basking in their popularity, Cook and Glaspell disbanded the company and moved on to Greece, convinced that acceptance by the establishment signaled their failure as revolutionary artists. Though the Provincetown Players gave their last performance on December 14, 1929, this is still a theater, fully restored in 1997 and presenting plays by and for young people, as well as community playhouse–produced O'Neill works.

Next door is:

10. **137 MacDougal St.** Jack London, Upton Sinclair, Vachel Lindsay, Louis Untermeyer, Max Eastman, Theodore Dreiser, Lincoln Steffens, and Sinclair Lewis hashed over life theories at the Liberal Club, "A Meeting Place for Those Interested in New Ideas," founded in 1913 on the second floor of the house that once stood here. Margaret Sanger lectured the club on birth control, an on-premises organization called Heterodoxy worked to promote feminist causes, and cubist art was displayed on the walls.

Downstairs were Polly's Restaurant (run by Polly Holladay and Hippolyte Havel) and the radical Washington Square Book Shop, from which Liberal Club members more often borrowed than bought. Holladay, a staunch anarchist, refused to join even the Liberal Club, which, however bohemian, was still an "organization." The apoplectic Havel, who was on the editorial board of *The Masses* (see Stop 38), once shouted out at a meeting where fellow members were debating which contributions to accept: "Bourgeois pigs! Voting! Voting on poetry! Poetry is something from the soul! You can't vote on poetry!" When Floyd Dell pointed out to Havel that he had once made editorial selections for the radical magazine *Mother Earth,* Havel shot back, "Yes, but we didn't abide by the results!" Hugo Kalmar, a character in O'Neill's *The Iceman Cometh,* is purportedly based on Havel. In a previous incarnation, this building was the home of Nathaniel Currier (of Currier and Ives).

Turn left onto West 4th Street and continue to the corner of:

11. **Sixth Avenue and West 4th Street.** Eugene O'Neill, a heavy drinker, nightly frequented a bar called the Golden Swan (more familiarly known as the "Hell Hole" or "Bucket of Blood") where the recycling center now stands, and later used it as a setting for his play *The Iceman Cometh,* a play that was 12 years in the writing. The bar was patronized by prostitutes, gangsters, longshoremen, anarchists, and politicians, as well as artists and writers. Eccentric owner Tom Wallace, on whom O'Neill modeled saloon proprietor Harry Hope, kept a pig in the basement and seldom ventured off the premises.

Cross Sixth Avenue, angle up the continuation of West 4th Street, and make your first left onto Cornelia Street looking for:

12. **33 Cornelia St.** Throughout the 1940s, film critic/poet/ novelist/screenwriter James Agee lived on Bleecker Street and worked in a studio at this address. Here he completed final revisions on *Let Us Now Praise Famous Men,* which portrayed the bleak lives of Alabama sharecroppers. The book originated in 1936 as an article for Henry Luce's *Fortune* magazine, which rejected the piece as too long and too liberal—the book's first pages contain a paraphrase from Marx's *Communist Manifesto:* "Workers of the world, unite and fight. You have nothing to lose but your chains, and a world to win."

Though a Harvard grad from an upper-class background, Agee was extremely sympathetic to the plight of the poor (he once took a hobo into his home); dubious, if not downright cynical, about the very nature of journalism; and ashamed of the intrusive nature of his mission. "It seems to me," he wrote, "obscene and thoroughly terrifying . . . to pry intimately into the lives of an undefended and appallingly damaged group of human beings, an ignorant and helpless rural family, for the purpose of parading the nakedness, disadvantage, and humiliation of these lives before another group of human beings, in the name of . . . honest journalism."

Nearby, at 31 Cornelia St., once stood the **Caffè Cino,** which opened in 1958, serving cappuccino in shaving mugs.

In the early 1960s, owner Joe Cino encouraged aspiring playwrights, such as Lanford Wilson, Sam Shepard, and John Guare, to stage readings and performances in his cramped storefront space. Experimentation in this tiny cafe gave birth to New York's off-Broadway theater. Plagued by money troubles, Cino committed suicide in 1967; Caffè Cino closed a year later.

Continue down Cornelia Street to Bleeker Street and turn right. Cross Seventh Avenue and angle back to your left into Commerce Street. Near the corner stands:

13. **11 Commerce St.** Washington Irving wrote *The Legend of Sleepy Hollow* while living in this quaint three-story brick building. Born into a prosperous New York family, as an officer in the War of 1812 he penned biographies of naval heroes. In 1819, under the name Geoffrey Crayon, he wrote *The Sketch Book,* which contained the stories of *The Legend of Sleepy Hollow, Westminster Abbey,* and *Rip Van Winkle.* Irving was one of the elite New Yorkers who served on the planning commission for Central Park, and, from 1842 to 1846, was ambassador to Spain. He coined the phrase "the almighty dollar," and once observed that "A tart temper never mellows with age, and a sharp tongue is the only tool that grows keener with constant use."

Continue walking west on Commerce and turn left at Bedford Street to find:

14. **75½ Bedford St.** The narrowest house in the Village (a mere 9½ feet across), this unlikely three-story brick residence was built on the site of a former carriage alley in 1873. Pretty red-headed feminist poet Edna St. Vincent Millay, who arrived in the Village fresh from Vassar, lived here from 1923 (the year she won a Pulitzer Prize for her poetry) to 1925. Ever a favorite among Village intelligentsia, the vivacious Millay perhaps best expressed her youthful passion for life in the lines:

My candle burns at both ends;
It will not last the night;
But ah, my foes, and oh, my friends—
It gives a lovely light!

Other famous occupants of the narrow house have included a young Cary Grant and John Barrymore.

Return to Commerce Street, and turn left, where:

15. **The Cherry Lane Theatre,** nestled in a bend at 38 Commerce St., was founded in 1924 by Edna St. Vincent Millay. Famed scenic designer Cleon Throckmorton transformed the revolutionary-era building (originally a farm silo, later a brewery and a box factory) into a playhouse that presented works by Edward Albee, Samuel Beckett (*Waiting for Godot* and *Endgame* premiered here), Eugene Ionesco, Jean Genet, and Harold Pinter. In 1951, Judith Malina and Julian Beck founded the ultra-experimental Living Theatre on its premises. Before rising to megafame, Barbra Streisand worked as a Cherry Lane usher.

Continue around Commerce Street's bend to Barrow Street, where you turn right, then left back onto Bedford Street. A few doors up on the right is:

16. **Chumley's,** 86 Bedford St. (☎ 212/675-4449), opened in 1926 in a former blacksmith's shop. During Prohibition it was a speakeasy with a casino upstairs. Its convoluted entranceway with four steps up and four down (designed to slow police raiders), the lack of a sign outside, and a back door that opens on an alleyway are remnants of that era. Original owner Lee Chumley was a radical labor sympathizer who held secret meetings of the IWW on the premises. Chumley's has long been a writer's bar. Walls are lined with book jackets of works by famous patrons who, over the years, have included Edna St. Vincent Millay (she once lived upstairs), John Steinbeck, Eugene O' Neill, e.e. cummings, Edna Ferber, John Dos Passos, F. Scott Fitzgerald, Theodore Dreiser, William Faulkner, Gregory Corso, Norman Mailer, William Carlos Williams, Allen Ginsberg, Lionel Trilling, Harvey Fierstein, Calvin Trillin, and numerous others. Even the elusive J.D. Salinger hoisted a few at the bar here, and Simone de Beauvoir came by when she was in town. With its working fireplaces (converted blacksmith forges), wood-plank flooring, old carved-up oak tables, and amber lighting, Chumley's lacks nothing in the way of mellowed atmosphere. Think about returning for drinks or dinner. A blackboard menu features fresh pasta and grilled fish. Open nightly from 5pm to an arbitrary closing time, Chumley's also offers brunch on weekends from 11am to 4pm.

Continue up Bedford to Grove Street, named in the 19th century for its many gardens and groves, and make a right to:

17. **17 Grove St.** Parts of this picturesque wood-frame house date to the early 1800s. A friend of James Baldwin's lived here in the 1960s, and Baldwin frequently stayed at the house. Baldwin, whose fiery writings coincided with the inception of the civil rights movement, once said, "The most dangerous creation of any society is that man who has nothing to lose."

    Further along is:

18. **45 Grove St.** Originally a freestanding two-story building, this was, in the 19th century, one of the Village's most elegant mansions, surrounded by verdant lawns with greenhouses and stables. Built in 1830, it was refurbished with Italianate influences in 1870. In the movie *Reds,* based on the life of John Reed, 45 Grove was portrayed (inaccurately) as Eugene O'Neill's house.

    Ohio-born poet Hart Crane rented a second-floor room at 45 Grove in 1923, and began writing his poetic portrait of America, *The Bridge* (Hart depicted the Brooklyn Bridge as a symbol of America's westward expansion). Crane was born in 1899 with "a toe in the 19th century." His parents' marriage was a miserably unhappy one, and his mother, an artistic beauty subject to depression, concentrated her aesthetic energies on her son, giving him music and dancing lessons, taking him to art galleries, and providing him with every kind of children's book and classic. Although constant traveling by his mother's side kept Crane from finishing school, he was a voracious reader and brilliantly self-educated. By the time he was 17, his poetry had been published in prestigious New York magazines and Nobel Prize–winning Indian poet Rabindranath Tagore was so impressed he arranged to meet Crane when visiting Cleveland.

    In later years, frustrated by frequent rejection from magazines and other exigencies of his craft, Crane would occasionally toss his typewriter out the window. Often moody and despondent, he was chronically in debt, plagued by guilt over homosexual encounters on the nearby docks, and given to almost nightly alcoholic binges; fellow Villager e.e. cummings once found him passed out on a sidewalk, bundled him into a taxi, and had him driven home. In 1932, returning by ship from Mexico (where, on a Guggenheim fellowship, he had been attempting to write an epic poem about Montezuma), Crane made sexual advances to a crew member, was badly beaten up, and jumped into the waters to his death at the age of 33.

Continue up the street to:

19. **59 Grove St.** English-born American revolutionary/ political theorist/writer Thomas Paine died here in 1809. Paine came to America (with the help of Benjamin Franklin) in 1774, and in 1776 produced his famous pamphlet, *The Crisis,* which begins with the words: "These are the times that try men's souls." After fighting in the American Revolution, he returned to England to advocate the overthrow of the British monarchy. Indicted for treason, he escaped to Paris, becoming a French citizen; while imprisoned there during the Terror, he wrote *The Age of Reason.* He returned to the United States in 1802, where he was vilified for his atheism. Benjamin Franklin once said to Paine, "Where liberty is, there is my country." To which revolutionary Paine replied: "Where liberty is not, there is mine."

The downstairs space has always been a restaurant, today **Marie's Crisis Cafe** (☎ 212/243-9323). Though the building Paine lived in burned down, some of the interior brickwork is original. Of note, behind the bar, is a WPA-era mural depicting the French and American Revolutions. Up a flight of stairs is another mural (a wood-relief carving) called *La Convention,* depicting Robespierre, Danton, and Thomas Paine. In the 1920s, you might have spotted anyone from Eugene O'Neill to Edward VIII of England here. Today, Marie's is a lively piano bar (everyone sings along nightly from 9:30pm to 3:30am).

At 7th Avenue, cross to the opposite side of the wide intersection, walk around to the left of the little park, and head half a block up Christopher Street, the hub of New York's gay community, to no. 53:

20. **The Stonewall.** The current bar in this spot shares a name with its more famous predecessor, the Stonewall Inn. This was scene of the Stonewall riots of June 1969, when gay customers decided to resist the police during a routine raid.

The event launched the lesbian and gay rights movement, and is commemorated throughout the country every year with gay pride parades. In the tiny Sheridan Square Park you just skirted, several of George Segal's realist sculptures honor the gay community. By portraying same-sex couples enjoying the park just like anybody else would, these sculptures point to the ludicrousness of marginalizing gay members of the park.

Continue up the block to the corner of:

21. **Waverly Place & Christopher Street.** The wedge-shaped Georgian Northern Dispensary building dates from 1831. Edgar Allan Poe was treated for a head cold here in 1836, the year he came to New York with his 13-year-old bride for whom he would later compose the pain-filled requiems *Annabel Lee* and *Ulalume:*

I was a child and she was a child,
In this kingdom by the sea;
But we loved with a love that was more than love—
I and my Annabel Lee.

Keep walking up Christopher Street to take a right onto:

22. **Gay Street.** Famous residents of this tiny street (originally a stable alley) have included New York Mayor Jimmy Walker, who owned the 18th-century town house at no. 12. More recently, Frank Paris, creator of *Howdy Doody,* lived here.

In the 1920s, Ruth McKenney lived in the basement of no. 14 with her sister Eileen, who later married Nathanael West. It was the setting for McKenney's zany *My Sister Eileen* stories, which were first published in the *New Yorker,* then collected into a book. They were then turned into a popular stage comedy that ran on Broadway from 1940 to 1942, followed by a Broadway musical version called *Wonderful Town* and two movie versions, one of them starring Rosalind Russell. The house dates from 1827.

Mary McCarthy, the *Partisan Review*'s drama critic and author of *The Stones of Florence* and *The Group,* lived in a studio apartment at no. 18 in the 1940s. During Prohibition there were several speakeasies on the street.

At the end of the short street, take a left into Waverly Place and look for:

23. **139 Waverly Place.** Edna St. Vincent Millay lived here with her sister, Norma, in 1918. Radical playwright Floyd Dell, her lover, who found the apartment for her, commented: "She lived in that gay poverty which is traditional of the Village, and one may find vivid reminiscences of that life in her poetry." An interesting note: Edna St. Vincent Millay's middle name was derived from St. Vincent's Hospital, which had saved the life of her uncle.

Cross Sixth Avenue to check out:

24. **116 Waverly Place.** Dating from 1891, the building has hosted William Cullen Bryant, Horace Greeley, Margaret Fuller, poet Fitz-Greene Halleck, and Herman Melville. Here Poe read his latest poem, *The Raven,* to assembled literati. Waverly Place, by the way, was named in 1833 for Sir Walter Scott's novel, *Waverley.*

Return to Sixth Avenue and turn left (south) down it. Take another left onto Washington Place to:

25. **82 Washington Place,** residence from 1908 to 1912 of Willa Cather, whose books celebrated pioneer life and the beauty of her native Nebraska landscape. Cather came to New York in 1906 at the age of 31 to work at the prestigious *McClure's* magazine and rose to managing editor before resigning to write full time. As her career advanced, and she found herself besieged with requests for lectures and interviews, Cather became almost reclusive and fiercely protective of her privacy. She complained,

> *In this country, a writer has to hide and lie and almost steal in order to get time to work in—and peace of mind to work with . . . . If we lecture, we get a little more owlish and self-satisfied all the time. We hate it at first, if we are decently modest, but in the end we fall in love with the sound of our own voice. There is something insidious about it, destructive to one's finer feelings. . . . It's especially destructive to writers, ever so much worse than alcohol, it takes their edge off.*

Band leader John Philip Sousa owned the beautiful 1839 building next door (no. 80).

Washington Place ends at:

26. **Washington Square Park,** the hub of the Village. This area was once a swamp frequented largely by duck hunters. Minetta Brook meandered through it. In the 18th and early

19th centuries it was a potter's field (more than 10,000 people are buried under the park) and an execution site (one of the makeshift gallows survives—a towering English elm in the northwest corner of the park). The park was dedicated in 1826, and elegant residential dwellings—some of which have survived NYU's cannibalization of the neighborhood—went up around the square. Rather than the center of Bohemia which it later became, it was the citadel of stifling patrician gentility so evocatively depicted in the novels of Edith Wharton. She defined Washington Square society as "a little 'set' with its private catch-words, observances and amusements" indifferent to "anything outside its charmed circle."

The white marble Memorial Arch (1892) at the Fifth Avenue entrance, which replaced a wooden arch erected in 1889 to commemorate the centenary of Washington's inauguration, was designed by Stanford White. One night in 1917, a group of Liberal Club pranksters climbed the Washington Square Arch, fired cap guns, and proclaimed the "independent republic of Greenwich Village," an utopia dedicated to "socialism, sex, poetry, conversation, dawn-greeting, anything—so long as it is taboo in the Middle West." Today, Washington Square Park would probably surpass any of this group's most cherished anarchist fantasies and might even lead them to question the philosophy altogether.

Along the square's north edge stand many of the surviving old homes, including, just west of Fifth Avenue:

27. 19 Washington Square North (Waverly Place).

Henry James's grandmother, Elizabeth Walsh, lived at this now-defunct address. (The no. 19 that exists today is a different house, the numbering system having changed since James's day.) Young Henry spent much time at her house—the inspiration for his novel *Washington Square,* later made into the Olivia de Havilland movie *The Heiress.* In 1875, James moved to Europe where he became an expert on expatriatism and penned many novels about Americans living abroad.

Further east is:

28. 7 Washington Square North, where Edith Wharton, age 20, and her mother lived in 1882. A wealthy aristocrat, born Edith Jones, Wharton maintained a close

friendship with Henry James, and, like him, left New York's stultifying upper-class social scene for Europe (Paris) in 1910, where she wrote the Pulitzer Prize–winning *The Age of Innocence.* Both she and James were immensely popular in Europe, deluged with invitations (James once admitted to accepting 107 dinner invitations in a single year). Wharton wrote almost a book a year her entire adult life, while also finding time to feed French and Belgian refugees during World War I and take charge of 600 Belgian orphans. For these efforts she was awarded the Legion of Honor by the French government in 1915. No. 7 was also once the home of Alexander Hamilton.

Nearby is:

29. **3 Washington Square North** (today the NYU School of Social Work). Critic Edmund Wilson, managing editor of the *New Republic,* lived here from 1921 to 1923. Another resident, John Dos Passos, wrote *Manhattan Transfer* here. Dos Passos, a fiery New York radical in the 1920s, became disillusioned with Communism after journeying to Spain with Hemingway during the Spanish Civil War. He was appalled that the Marxist-backed Republicans executed his friend Jose Robles, himself a Republican supporter. The incident, which also caused a break between Dos Passos and Hemingway when the latter refused to challenge the integrity of the Republican cause, was the basis of Dos Passos's next novel, *Adventures of a Young Man* (1939). His books thereafter also demonstrated a marked shift to the right. In the 1940s, Dos Passos returned to his native Virginia.

Make a left at University Place and another immediate left into:

30. **Washington Mews.** This picturesque 19th-century cobblestoned street, lined with vine-covered two-story buildings (converted stables and carriage houses constructed to serve posh Washington Square town houses), has had several famous residents, among them John Dos Passos, artist Edward Hopper (no. 14A), and Sherwood Anderson (no. 54). The latter building dates from 1834.

Double back to University Place and turn left to head north to the southeast corner of 9th Street, where stands the first of two possible places to:

Take a Break The more expensive and formal of choices is the **Knickerbocker Bar and Grill** (☎ 212/ 228-8490) at the southeast corner of 9th Street and University Place. It is a comfortable wood-paneled restaurant and jazz club that attracts an interesting clientele including writers (Jack Newfield, E.L. Doctorow, Erica Jong, Sidney Zion, Christopher Cerf) and actors (Richard Gere, F. Murray Abraham, Susan Sarandon, Tim Robbins). Harry Connick Jr. got his start playing piano at the Knickerbocker, and Charles Lindbergh signed the contract for his transatlantic flight at the bar here. The restaurant is open daily for lunch/brunch from 11:45am; an eclectic menu offers entrées ranging from pasta dishes to bangers and mash to Southwestern paella.

For smaller appetites, head two blocks up to a branch of **Dean and Deluca,** 75 University Place, at 11th Street (☎ 212/473-1908). They offer superior light fare— pastries, croissants, ham and brie sandwiches on baguette, pasta salads—in a pristinely charming setting, usually enhanced by classical music. Be sure to look up at the gorgeous plasterwork ceiling. Open Monday to Thursday 8am to 10pm, Friday and Saturday 8am to 11pm, and Sunday 9am to 8pm.

This address is also a stop on the tour. When Thomas Wolfe graduated from Harvard in 1923, he came to New York to teach at NYU and lived at the Hotel Albert (depicted as the Hotel Leopold in his novel *Of Time and the River*) at this address. Today the Albert Apartments occupy the site.

From University Place, turn left onto 11th Street to:

31. **25 East 11th St.** The unhappy and sexually confused poet Hart Crane (whom we met at Stop 18) lived here for a short time. His neighbor at:

32. **21 East 11th St.** was Mary Cadwaller Jones, who was married to Edith Wharton's brother. Her home was the setting of literary salons; Henry Adams, Theodore Roosevelt, Augustus Saint-Gaudens, and John Singer Sargent often came to lunch, and Henry James was a houseguest when he visited America from Europe. Jones's daughter, landscape architect Baetrix Farrand, grew up here before designing such renowned outdoor spaces as the White House's

East Garden and the New York Botanical Gardens' Rose Garden.

Continue to Fifth Avenue, cross it, and turn right. On your left is:

33. **The Salmagundi Club,** 47 Fifth Ave., which began as an artist's club in 1871 and was originally located at 596 Broadway. The name comes from the *Salmagundi* papers, in which Washington Irving mocked his fellow New Yorkers and first used the term *Gotham* to describe the city. *Salmagundi*, which means "a stew of many ingredients," was thought an appropriate term to describe the club's diverse membership—painters, sculptors, writers, and musicians. The club moved to this mid–19th-century brownstone mansion in 1917. Theodore Dreiser lived at the Salmagundi in 1897, when it was located across the street where today stands the First Presbyterian Church, and probably wrote *Sister Carrie* there, a work based on the experiences of his own sister, Emma.

Cross 12th Street. At the northwest corner is:

34. **The Forbes Magazine Building,** 60–62 Fifth Ave., with a museum (☎ 212/206-5548) housing exhibits from the varied collections of the late Malcolm Forbes, famous as a frequent Liz Taylor escort, financier, magazine magnate, and father of one-time Presidential hopeful Steve Forbes. On display are hundreds of model ships; legions formed from a collection of more than 100,000 military miniatures; thousands of signed letters, papers, and other paraphernalia from almost every American president; a remarkable even dozen of Fabergé eggs and other objets d'art fashioned for the czars; the evolution of the game Monopoly (natch); and changing exhibits and art shows. Admission is free. The galleries are open Tuesday to Saturday 10am to 4pm.

Make a left on 12th Street and you'll see.

35. **The New School for Social Research,** 66 West 12th St., which was founded in 1919 as a forum for professors too liberal-minded for Columbia University's then stiflingly traditional attitude. In the 1930s it became a "University in Exile" for intelligentsia fleeing Nazi Germany. Many great writers have taught or lectured in its classrooms over the decades—William Styron, Joseph Heller, Edward Albee,

W.H. Auden, Robert Frost, Nadine Gordimer, Max Lerner, Maya Angelou, Joyce Carol Oates, Arthur Miller, I.B. Singer, Susan Sontag, and numerous others.

Turn right up Sixth Avenue and left onto 13th Street to:

36. **138 West 13th St.** Max Eastman and other radicals urged revolution in the pages of the *Liberator,* headquartered in this lovely building on a pleasant tree-lined street. The magazine published works by John Reed, Edna St. Vincent Millay, Ernest Hemingway, Elinor Wylie, e.e. cummings (who later became very right-wing and a passionate supporter of Sen. Joseph McCarthy's Communist witch hunts), John Dos Passos, and William Carlos Williams. The *Liberator,* established in 1919, succeeded *The Masses,* an earlier Eastman publication (see Stop 38).

Further west along the block is:

37. **152 West 13th St.** Offices of the *Dial,* a major avant-garde literary magazine of the 1920s, occupied this beautiful Greek Revival brick town house. The magazine dated from 1840 in Cambridge, Massachusetts, where transcendentalists Margaret Fuller and Ralph Waldo Emerson were its seminal editors. In the '20s, its aim was to offer "the best of European and American art, experimental and conventional." Contributors included Marianne Moore, Hart Crane, Conrad Aiken, Ezra Pound, Theodore Dreiser (who once wrote an article claiming that American literature had to be crude to be truly American), and artist Marc Chagall. T.S. Eliot, who once grumbled of the *Dial* "there is far too much in it, and it is all second rate and exceedingly solemn," nevertheless published *The Waste Land* in its pages.

Continue west on 13th Street, and make a left on Seventh Avenue, a right on 12th Street, and then another right for some afternoon tea.

Take a Break When Londoner Nicky Perry moved to New York, she was disappointed to find no proper British tea houses where she could get a decent cup of tea, so she opened her own in 1990. **Tea and Sympathy** (☎ 212/807-8329), at 108 Greenwich Ave., is straight out of the English countryside, a hole-in-the-wall crammed with a few tables (always crowded), a friendly British wait staff, and plenty of old-time charm in the form of

Anglo-paraphernalia plastered over the walls. Elbow room is at a minimum here, but it's worth the squeeze for a $14 full afternoon tea—a tiered serving tray stuffed full of finger sandwiches with the crusts cut off (cucumber-and-mayo or egg salad), cakes, biscuits, scones, jam, and clotted cream, plus, of course, a pot of tea (go for the Typhoo). Cheaper, bona fide British dishes include shepherd's pie, bangers and mash, and Welsh rarebit. For dessert, try a treacle pudding or warm ginger cake. Tea and Sympathy is open daily from 11:30am to 10:30pm.

From Tea and Sympathy, turn left to walk back down Greenwich Avenue to the corner of 12th Street and:

38. **91 Greenwich Ave.** At the beginning of the 20th century, Max Eastman was editor of a radical left-wing literary magazine called *The Masses*. This magazine published, among others, John Reed, Carl Sandburg, Sherwood Anderson, Upton Sinclair, Edgar Lee Masters, e.e. cummings, and Louis Untermeyer. John Sloan, Stuart Davis, Picasso, and George Bellows provided art for its pages, which a newspaper columnist dismissed thusly:

They draw nude women for The Masses,
Thick, fat, ungainly lasses—
How does that help the working classes?

Reed wrote the magazine's statement of purpose: "To everlastingly attack old systems, old morals, old prejudices." *The Masses* was suppressed by the Justice Department in 1918 because of its opposition to World War I (it called on Woodrow Wilson to repeal the draft and claimed that America's enemy was not Germany but "that 2 percent of the United States that owns 60 percent of all the wealth"). Reed, Eastman, political cartoonist Art Young, and writer/literary critic Floyd Dell were put on trial under the Espionage Act and charged with conspiracy to obstruct recruiting and prevent enlistment. Pacifist Edna St. Vincent Millay read poems to the accused to help pass the time while juries were out. The trials all ended in hung juries.

Continue another block down Greenwich Avenue; turn right on Bank Street, and look for:

39. **1 Bank St.** In 1913, shortly after the publication of *O Pioneers!*, Willa Cather, age 40, moved to a seven-room,

second-floor apartment in a large brick house here. Here she lived with her companion Edith Lewis and wrote *My Antonia* (the third of a trilogy about immigrants in the United States), *Death Comes to the Archbishop,* and several other novels. In 1920, H.L. Mencken called *My Antonia* "the best piece of fiction ever done by a woman in America . . . I know of no novel that makes the remote folk of the western farmlands more real than *My Antonia* makes them, and know of none that makes them seem better worth knowing."

When she became successful, Cather rented the apartment above hers and kept it empty to ensure perfect quiet. Her Friday afternoon at-homes here were frequented by D.H. Lawrence, among others. Unlike many Village writers of her day, Cather eschewed the radical scene and took little interest in politics.

From Bank Street, take a left onto Waverly Place, another left on Perry Street, and a final right back onto Greenwich Avenue, to:

40. **45 Greenwich Ave.** In 1947, William Styron came to New York from North Carolina to work as a junior editor at McGraw-Hill. He moved here in 1951, after a stint in the marines and the success of his first novel, *Lie Down in Darkness.* Styron originally showed manuscript pages from that novel, begun at age 23, to Hiram Haydn, a Bobbs-Merrill editor whose writing class he was taking at the New School. Haydn told Styron he was too advanced for the class and took an option on the novel.

Continue down Greenwich Avenue to West 10th Street and detour right to:

41. **139 West 10th St.** Today an Italian restaurant, this was the site, for decades, of a popular Village bar called the Ninth Circle. But it was at a former bar at this location that, in 1954, playwright Edward Albee saw graffiti on a mirror reading, "Who's afraid of Virginia Woolf?" and, years later, appropriated it. He recalled the incident in a *Paris Review* interview: "When I started to write the play it cropped up in my mind again. And of course, Who's Afraid of Virginia Woolf means . . . who's afraid of living life without false illusions."

Double back up West 10th Street, cross Greenwich Avenue, and walk a block where you will see the gated entry to:

42. **Patchin Place.** The gate closing off Patchin Place is never locked; feel free to pass through it. This tranquil, tree-shaded cul-de-sac has sheltered many illustrious residents: From 1923 to 1962, e.e. cummings lived at no. 4, where visitors included T.S. Eliot, Ezra Pound, and Dylan Thomas. The highly acclaimed but little-known Djuna Barnes (literary critics have compared her to James Joyce) lived in a tiny one-room apartment at no. 5. Reclusive and eccentric, she almost never left the premises for 40 years, prompting cummings to occasionally shout from his window, "Are you still alive, Djuna?"

Among other works, Barnes wrote a memoir called *Life Is Painful, Nasty, & Short . . . In My Case It Has Only Been Nasty* (it certainly wasn't short; she lived to the age of 90); an experimental poetic novel called *Nightwood* (for which T. S. Eliot penned an introduction); and a collection of poetry called *The Book of Repulsive Women*. Three of her one-act plays were produced at the Provincetown Playhouse in 1919 and 1920.

Though they were usually elsewhere, John Reed and Louise Bryant maintained a residence at Patchin Place from 1895 until his death in 1920. It was during this time that he wrote his eyewitness account of the Russian Revolution, *Ten Days That Shook the World.* To avoid interruptions from callers at Patchin Place, Reed rented a room atop a restaurant at 147 West 4th Street to do his writing. Theodore Dreiser and John Masefield were also Patchin Place residents, the former in 1895 when he was still an unknown journalist.

Turn left out of Patchin Place to cross Sixth Avenue. We'll be continuing down West 10th Street, but look to your right as you cross Sixth Avenue to see the:

43. **Jefferson Market Library** at 425 Sixth Ave., a former produce market. The turreted red-brick and granite Victorian-Gothic castle was built as a courthouse in 1877 and named for Thomas Jefferson. Topped by a lofty clock/bell tower (originally intended as a fire lookout), with traceried

and stained-glass windows, gables, and steeply sloping roofs, the building was inspired by a Bavarian castle. In the 1880s, architects voted it one of the 10 most beautiful buildings in America.

Head east down 10th Street to:

44. **50 West 10th St.** After his great success with *Who's Afraid of Virginia Woolf?*, Edward Albee bought this late 19th-century converted carriage house in the early 1960s. It's a gem of a building, with highly polished wooden carriage doors. Albee wrote *Tiny Alice* and *A Delicate Balance* here, the latter a Pulitzer Prize winner. In 1994, he won a second Pulitzer Prize for *Three Tall Women*.

Now look for:

45. **37 West 10th St.** Sinclair Lewis, already a famous writer by the mid-1920s, lived in this early 19th-century house with his wife, journalist Dorothy Thompson, from 1928 to 1929. Lewis fell in love with the recently divorced Thompson at first sight in 1927, and immediately proposed to her. Once, when asked to speak at a dinner party he stood up and said, "Dorothy, will you marry me?" and resumed his seat. Lewis later followed her to Russia and all over Europe until she accepted his proposal. Unfortunately, the marriage didn't last.

Our final stop is:

46. **14 West 10th St.** When Mark Twain came to New York at the turn of the century (at the age of 65), he lived in this gorgeous 1855 mansion. An extremely successful writer, he entertained lavishly. Born Samuel Langhorne Clemens, Twain, a one-time riverboat captain, took his pseudonym from a river calling that warned of shallow waters ("mark twain" means "by the mark two fathoms"). Twain was famous for his witticisms, including a quip on the art of quipping: "How lucky Adam was. He knew when he said a good thing, nobody had said it before."

The East Village

Start: The Strand Bookstore, at the intersection of Broadway and 12th Street.

Subway: Take the 4, 5, 6, N, or R to 14th Street/Union Square station; walk south on Broadway.

Finish: Astor Place subway kiosk.

Time: 3 to 5 hours.

Best Time: Weekdays after 9:30am, when the Strand has opened.

Worst Time: Weekends, when some places may be closed; however, even then there's plenty to see.

Like other New York City neighborhoods, the East Village has reinvented itself time and time again in the years between its inception as part of Dutch governor Peter Stuyvesant's farm and its current incarnation as the funky fringe of the city's arts and nightlife scene. From about 1840, one immigrant enclave after another filled the neighborhood's town houses and tenements, and all of these people have left their stamp—from the early Irish and German settlers to the still-extant mix of Jews, African Americans, Latin Americans, Japanese, Indians, Eastern Europeans (especially Ukrainians), and Italians. In that melting pot boils an important ingredient—latter-day-bohemian middle-class refuseniks who still arrive here daily from all over the country. This diversity is the East Village's defining characteristic.

In the 1960s and '70s, the neighborhood was the hub of hippiedom. The action then centered on St. Mark's Place between Second and Third avenues where Abbie Hoffman lived. Other major players included Allen Ginsberg, Jerry Rubin, Timothy Leary, cartoonist R. Crumb, Paul Krassner (editor of *The Realist*), Andy Warhol, concert promoter Bill Graham, and an assortment of Indian swamis, witches and warlocks, tarot card readers, Hell's Angels, Hare Krishnas, flower children, and political radicals. East Villagers of those decades ate macrobiotic, took yoga, and lived in $30-a-month railroad flats with bathtubs in the kitchen (barely renovated, these apartments now rent for $1,000 a month). They thrilled to Janis Joplin and the Grateful Dead at the Fillmore East, danced at Warhol's Electric Circus, listened to jazz at the Five Spot, read the *East Village Other* and the Bhagavad Gita, and took in three-for-a-dollar features at the St. Mark's Cinema.

In the 1980s, the East Village took a stab at becoming the next SoHo, complete with chic galleries and nightclubs, co-op conversions, and escalating rents. A declining economy toward the end of the decade seems to have rendered the nascent art scene stillborn, but trendy clubs and upscale restaurants are still thriving in the '90s. Hippies have been replaced by spike-haired punks, anarchists, and crack dealers—as well as youthful yuppie types who either can't yet afford uptown rents or simply enjoy the action of this ever-vibrant area. Old-time residents still find it jarring to see the suit-and-tie set hoisting beers at the local bars. But gentrification notwithstanding, the East Village remains one of New York's most vital districts, a last holdout of bohemianism.

• • • • • • • • • • • • • • • •

Begin your tour at the northeast corner of Broadway and 12th Street, where you will see a beehive of activity surrounding the:

1. **Strand Bookstore** (☎ 212/473-1452). This is the world's largest used bookstore and one of New York's most cherished institutions. The last survivor of Fourth Avenue's old Book Row, the Strand—named for the famous London

The East Village

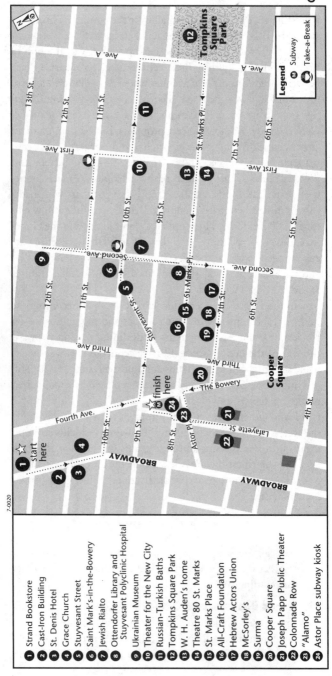

1. Strand Bookstore
2. Cast-Iron Building
3. St. Denis Hotel
4. Grace Church
5. Stuyvesant Street
6. Saint Mark's-in-the-Bowery
7. Jewish Rialto
8. Ottendorfer Library and Stuyvesant Polyclinic Hospital
9. Ukrainian Museum
10. Theater for the New City
11. Russian-Turkish Baths
12. Tompkins Square Park
13. W. H. Auden's home
14. Theatre 80 St. Marks
15. St. Marks Place
16. All-Craft Foundation
17. Hebrew Actors Union
18. McSorley's
19. Surma
20. Cooper Square
21. Joseph Papp Public Theater
22. Colonnade Row
23. "Alamo"
24. Astor Place subway kiosk

street—was founded by Benjamin Bass in 1929. Today run by his son, Fred Bass, and Fred's daughter Nancy, it continues to be a favorite haunt of the city's rumpled intellectuals. Lee Strasberg, Anaîs Nin, and Andy Warhol were all regular customers during their lifetimes. Saul Bellow stops by when he's in town. The store has stayed open late so that Michael Jackson could peruse vintage children's books in privacy, and Sophia Loren once waited in a car outside while she sent Anna Strasberg to pick up books for her. It's a bit of a madhouse at times, a maze of narrow aisles threading past towering stacks of books shelved haphazardly within their categories, but for die-hard book lovers, it all only adds to the treasure hunt.

"Every book," says Bass, "eventually turns up here." The store boasts "eight miles of books." At any given time its inventory comprises more than 2 million tomes, a variety on every subject you can imagine at bargain basement prices, including remainders, reviewer copies (sold at half price), used paperbacks, great art books, and hard-to-find novels. On the third floor is a huge collection of rare books where you might run across a second folio Shakespeare for $50,000, a first edition of *Uncle Tom's Cabin* for $2,500, or *The Story of the Exodus* with original Marc Chagall lithographs for $35,000. You can also find signed first editions (some for as little as $15). The Strand is open 9:30am to 9:30pm Monday to Saturday, 11am to 9:30pm Sundays.

Walk downtown on Broadway to 11th Street. On the northwest corner is the:

2. **Cast-Iron Building.** Cast-iron architecture was the vogue in New York throughout the latter half of the 19th century, providing an economical means of embellishing buildings with ornate, often neoclassical facades. This one, constructed in 1868 to house the James McCreery Dry Goods Store, is one of the few buildings left standing from the stretch of Broadway between 23rd and 8th streets that became known after the Civil War as "Ladies' Mile."

Luxury hotels and elegant department stores such as Wanamaker's, B. Altman, and Lord and Taylor opened up in this area; by the 1870s and 1880s, the high society of New York's Gilded Age enjoyed a splendor unrivaled in the New World. As writer Robert Macoy boasted in 1876,

Broadway was "the grand promenade and swarm[ed] with the beauty, fashion, and wealth of New York. No avenue or street in London or Paris or Berlin, or any of our cities, can be compared with it." Toward the end of the 19th century, New York's wealthy families moved uptown, creating fashionable neighborhoods along Park, Madison, and Fifth Avenues, and Ladies' Mile went into decline.

When McCreery's moved uptown in 1913, the Cast-Iron Building was converted first to office and warehouse space, then in 1971 to apartments. McCreery, an Irish immigrant who became a major New York merchandiser, was a patron of the arts, leaving much of his fortune to the Metropolitan Museum.

Across 11th Street on the southwest corner of the intersection is the building that used to house the:

3. **St. Denis Hotel.** Opened in 1848, the St. Denis for 60 years offered the pinnacle of luxury and fashion to visitors. Famous guests included everyone from Abraham Lincoln to eminent Parisian actress Sarah Bernhardt. In 1877, Alexander Graham Bell demonstrated his recently patented telephone to New York notables here (he called someone in Brooklyn). Today the building's exterior is undistinguished. Much like the Cast-Iron Building—which was robbed of its lovely mansard roof when developers replaced it with a stolid two-story addition of apartments—the St. Denis suffered injury as well as insult during Broadway's decline. All of the ornamentation that once graced the exterior was removed in 1917 when the St. Denis was converted to office space. If you walk around the corner on 11th Street, you can see some more of the surviving facade on both of these buildings from another angle.

Continuing downtown on Broadway, immediately on your left is:

4. **Grace Church.** One of the finest examples of Gothic Revival architecture in the United States, Grace Church was built between 1843 and 1847. It was the first masterpiece of 23-year-old architect James Renwick Jr., who would go on to design St. Patrick's Cathedral and the Smithsonian "castle." Renwick was also a regular parishioner, and his bust graces the west corner of the north transept. The garden in front of the parish house and rectory on Broadway

Tom Thumb Ties the Knot

Despite its stunning architecture and traditional upper-class congregation, the most famous event ever to occur at Grace Church was a less than dignified one. P.T. Barnum arranged for the nuptials of two of his "biggest" sideshow stars, the diminutive Gen. Tom Thumb and his like-sized bride Lavinia Warren, to be celebrated at the church. Though attended by the cream of society, their 1863 wedding exhibited all of the rowdiness and hoopla of a typical Barnum production. A parishioner who challenged sexton Isaac Hull Brown about the propriety of the affair received the response: "Even little people have the right to marry in a big church."

was created by Calvert Vaux, who helped designed Central Park.

In the middle of the 19th century, this was the most fashionable church in New York, with reserved pew seating costing $1,200 to $1,400, and always booked full of weddings. Former New York City Mayor Philip Hone wrote in his *Diary* that the stiff price of pews "may have a good effect; for many of them, though rich, know how to calculate, and if they do not go regularly to Church, they will not get the worth of their money." He described the aisles of the church as filled with "gay parties of ladies in feathers and mousseline-de-laine dresses, and dandies with moustaches and high heeled boots."

In his opening sermon at Grace Church, Dr. Thomas House Taylor exclaimed, "I do not believe that the commonest laborer who has wrought on these stones can ever look back upon his work without a feeling of reverence and awe." The church is laden with stone carvings, the pulpit is of carved oak, and from the handsome mosaic floors rise lofty columns to support the vaulted ceiling. The building is constructed of hewn white marble and its slender marble spire, atop a 110-foot tower, dramatically marks the horizon. Over the main entrance is a large, circular stained-glass window, and 45 additional interior Gothic windows sparkle with richly hued stained glass. Though all merit attention, note especially the five pre-Raphaelite windows by Henry Holiday along the north and south aisles of the nave depicting "Ruth and Naomi," "Joseph and Benjamin," "The Raising of Lazarus," "The Raising of Jairus' Daughter," and "The Four Marys."

The church is open 10am to 5:45pm weekdays, Saturday noon to 4pm, Sunday during services only from 8am. For information on church programs, organ concerts, and services, call ☎ 212/254-2000.

Follow the perimeter of the church grounds around to Fourth Avenue between 10th and 11th streets to see the trio of houses built decades later in a Gothic Revival style faithful to the church itself. The northern of the trio, the **Grace Memorial House,** was designed by Renwick himself, whereas the others were designed by his firm.

Turn around to make your way south on Fourth Avenue. At 9th Street, you'll see looming over the southwest corner of Fourth Avenue and Wanamaker Place the **former Wanamaker Department Store Annex,** another Italianate cast-iron survivor from Ladies' Mile (now a K-mart).

Turn left to walk east on 9th Street, cross Third Avenue, and bear left onto the diagonal:

5. **Stuyvesant Street.** This street, one of the most charming in New York, is the namesake of the dour Dutch peg-legged governor of Nieuw Amsterdam, Peter Stuyvesant (1592–1672), who built a large *bouwerie* (farm) for himself here in the mid-1600s. Stuyvesant Street was the entrance to his property, extending all the way to the East River. The governor's descendants continued to reside in the area into the 19th century. When city officials decided in 1811 to impose the street grid that characterizes Manhattan today, the wealthy families here saved the street from being razed; it is one of the few true east-west streets in the city.

The stately edifices along this street are most famous as wealthy private homes from the mid–19th century. However, the early 20th century saw many of them doing a brisk business as brothels (in particular nos. 25, 27, 29, and 31).

No. 21, a wide Federal-style, three-story brick building known as the Stuyvesant-Fish House, was built in 1804 for the governor's great-great-granddaughter, Elizabeth, and her husband, Nicholas Fish, a Revolutionary War hero who had served at Valley Forge. Nicholas and Elizabeth's son,

A Costly Corpse

Although many illustrious persons decay under the cobblestones of St. Mark's-in-the-Bowery, the graveyard's most famous resident rested in peace here for only 2½ years.

When Manhattan mogul A.T. Stewart died in 1876, he left behind a mercantile legacy including the country's first department store (the Marble Dry Goods Palace) and a now vanished Cast Iron Palace along Ladies' Mile.

A notoriously cold-hearted man, Stewart also left behind a reputation of brutal ruthlessness, miserliness, cruelty toward his employees, and general, thin-lipped meanness. Posthumously called "one of the meanest men that ever lived," when alive, public outcry hastily forced President Grant to retract Stewart's name as appointee to Secretary of the Treasury.

In a feat of ironic justice, on the night of November 6, 1878, police reported that the merchant's rotting corpse had been yanked from its vault, dragged across the yard—leaving bits of A.T. Stewart as a grisly trail—and hauled over the fence.

In 1879, a ransom note demanded $200,000 for the remains. The police countered with an offer of $25,000, which the ransomers declined. In 1881, Stewart's widow reopened negotiations at $100,000, and eventually negotiated down to $20,000. The bones were quickly laid to rest in a vault of Garden City Cathedral on Long Island—this time, with an alarm system.

Although the thieves were never caught, many have concluded the crime was an inside job. The entrance to Stewart's vault had been moved and covered over with sod after an earlier theft attempt—no one knows if this first body-napping attempt was related. However, even though Stewart had recently been hidden under an unmarked spot in the ground, the tomb raiders wasted no time heading straight to the correct blank spot in the graveyard turf. The vault itself still exists, unmarked, underground. It is grave no. 112, near the yard's center, and you'll find the spot wedged between Winthrop's iron cross vault no. 11 and Bibby's red stone no. 113.

Hamilton, went on to become governor of New York, a U.S. senator, and secretary of state under President Grant.

Adjacent to the Stuyvesant-Fish House begins the Renwick Triangle, a group of 16 elegant brick-and-brownstone Anglo-Italianate town houses built in 1861 (nos. 23 to 35 on Stuyvesant Street and nos. 114 to 128 on 10th Street) and attributed to James Renwick. Architect Stanford White once lived at 118 East 10th St. You'll have to walk around the corner to see these 10th Street houses, but before you do, note the earliest house on Stuyvesant Street, no. 44, which was built in 1795 for Nicholas William Stuyvesant, a merchant. Its splayed lintels and Flemish bond brickwork are typical of the period, and the proportions of the doorway are an indication of this residence's original grandeur.

At the end of Stuyvesant Street, at 10th Street, is:

6. **Saint Mark's-in-the-Bowery.** This late-Georgian Episcopal stone church, completed in 1799, replaced the 1660 chapel that was part of Peter Stuyvesant's farm. To the left and right of the Italianate cast-iron portico are statues of Native Americans by Solon Borglum called "Aspiration" and "Inspiration" (Borglum's more famous brother, Gutzon, carved the heads at Mount Rushmore) and busts of Peter Stuyvesant and Daniel Tompkins.

Tompkins (vice president under Monroe and a former New York governor) is buried here in the cobblestoned courtyard, along with other prominent 18th- and 19th-century New Yorkers—among them, Mayor Philip Hone, several British colonial governors, Commodore Matthew Perry (who forced Japan to open diplomatic relations with the United States in the early 1850s), and Peter Stuyvesant himself—along with seven generations of his descendants. According to some accounts, there are even graves beyond the churchyard under Second Avenue.

St. Mark's Greek Revival steeple was added in 1828; its brick Parish Hall was designed by James Renwick in 1861 and its rectory by noted architect Ernest Flagg in 1900. To get a look at the interior, you have to call ahead for an appointment (☎ 212/674-6377) or attend a service or cultural event here. After a 1978 fire, the top stained-glass windows had to be replaced; the new windows depict life on the Lower East Side. The original bottom windows (including one depicting Peter Stuyvesant) remain intact. If the garden courtyards are open, walk in and browse around. Especially lovely is the west courtyard behind the church—a tranquil oasis with benches shaded by ancient maple and London plane trees.

For many decades, Saint Mark's has ardently supported the East Village arts community. Along with La Mama and Caffè Cino, it was a major birthplace of off-Broadway theater, nurturing playwrights such as Sam Shepard (whose first two plays, *Cowboys* and *Rock Garden,* were produced here). Another long-running church program is Danspace (Isadora Duncan danced here in the 1920s, Martha Graham in the 1930s, and more recently, Merce Cunningham). And the Poetry Project has featured readings by Kahlil Gibran, William Carlos Williams, Edna St. Vincent Millay, Carl Sandburg, Amy Lowell, Allen Ginsberg, and W.H. Auden (a member of the parish, he sometimes used to come to church in his bathrobe and slippers). Saint Mark's was also the setting for a wedding in the movie *The Group,* based on Mary McCarthy's best seller.

Take a Break There are numerous choices here. Diagonally across the street from the church is the famed **Second Avenue Deli**—a New York institution for more than 40 years, serving up Jewish soul food nonpareil. Everyone patronizes this deli; you might see anyone from comic Jackie Mason to politicos like Bella Abzug or Geraldine Ferraro at the next table. Mafia don John Gotti was a regular before his imprisonment, even sending for take-out during the trial. Stop in for authentic pastrami and corned beef piled high on fresh-baked rye, chopped liver, kasha varnishkes, knishes, and other deli favorites.

Or try the plain-Jane, inexpensive, and ultra-friendly **Ukrainian Restaurant,** 140 Second Ave. (on 9th Street), for Eastern European specialties such as blini, pierogi, potato pancakes, and borscht. The restaurant occupies the basement of the Ukrainian National Home. Incidentally, the Ukrainian National Home was the infamous Stuyvesant Casino in the early 20th century, meeting ground for the Lower East Side's criminal element. Gangsters would throw parties here, forcing local merchants both to buy tickets and to pay for ads in a souvenir booklet. The ensuing fetes tended to be rowdy and were nicknamed after the "racket" they raised. The term "racket" would eventually be applied to all illegal gangster revenue-raising activities, and racketeering became the. official crime they were committing.

Be sure to stop in front of the Second Avenue Deli where brass-lined plaques set into the sidewalk (and the interior Molly Pecon Room) commemorate Second Avenue's heyday as the:

7. **Jewish Rialto.** New York's Jewish community increased in number and prosperity in the early years of the 20th century, and the new Jewish middle class turned Second Avenue between Houston and 14th streets into a center of Yiddish culture. Dubbed the Yiddish Broadway, it was the site of cafes, bookstores, and a score of Yiddish-language theaters, many of them lasting until the 1950s. Actors such as Jacob Adler (father of noted drama teacher Stella Adler), and comic actors Menashe Skulnik, Boris and Bessie Thomashevsky, and Maurice Schwartz took the stage every night in "immigrant-makes-good" plays, melodramas, and stock Yiddish comedy situations transposed to an American setting. Jacob Adler spearheaded a more serious dramatic movement, becoming famous for his "improved and enlarged" portrayal of King Lear and his proud version of Shylock. Thomashevsky adapted Shakespeare and Goethe to the Yiddish stage, and such well-known actors as Paul Muni, Edward G. Robinson, and Walter Matthau came up through the Yiddish theater.

Across from the Ukrainian Restaurant, at 135–37 Second Avenue, are the:

8. **Ottendorfer Library and Stuyvesant Polyclinic Hospital.** These two ornately embellished redbrick facilities are the 1884 gift of Anna and Oswald Ottendorfer, publishers of a German-language daily newspaper called *Staats-Zeitung,* to the once-thriving Germany community of this neighborhood. Their aim was to nurture both the intellect and physical well-being of the immigrant population. Today the oldest extant branch of the New York City Public Library, the Ottendorfer's late Victorian building is adorned with terra-cotta wisdom symbols—globes,

books, scrolls, owls, and torches. Its original name, the Freie Bibliothek und Lesehall, is still chiseled into the facade.

The adjacent clinic, even more elaborately adorned, features portrait busts of Hippocrates, Celsius, Galen, Humboldt, Lavoisier, and other scientists and physicians. The clinic was originally named the German Dispensary, but its administrators attempted to deflect anti-German sentiment during World War I by changing its name to the Stuyvesant Polyclinic Hospital. Both buildings were designed by architect William Schickel.

Walk north on Second Avenue past 12th Street, and look for no. 203 on your left. The fourth and fifth floors of this building house the:

9. **Ukrainian Museum** (☎ 212/228-0110). This small museum is committed to preserving the cultural heritage of the Ukrainian people. An assortment of folk art items are on permanent display, including traditional costumes and textiles of intricate embroidery and needlework. You can also see exquisite *pysanky*, wax-resistant-decorated Easter eggs that, according to legend, will conquer evil if enough are painted. In ancient times, these were created only by women and young girls—in secret, lest someone cast an evil spell on the egg—using fertilized eggs of chickens that had laid for the first time. The museum also displays Ukrainian art, along with *rushnyky* (woven and embroidered ritual cloths traditionally used as talismans in births, weddings, funerals, and calendrical rites associated with the change of seasons), ceramics, and decorative brass and silver jewelry. The museum shop offers you the opportunity to buy examples of all the above, as well as egg-decorating kits. Courses in Ukrainian folk crafts are also offered. Hours are Wednesday to Sunday, 1 to 5pm. A small admission is charged.

Backtrack on Second Avenue to its intersection with 11th Street and turn left.

☕ **Take a Break** Eleventh Street between First and Second avenues is a little Little Italy, where a small Italian community still flourishes. Stop into **Veniero's Pasticceria** (☎ **212/674-7070**) at no. 342—this century-old Italian bakery and cafe is the perfect place for cannoli and cappuccino. Veniero's is charming, with old-fashioned tile floors, beveled mirrors, an ornate pressed-copper ceiling punctuated by stained-glass skylights, and marble cafe tables. Its vast display cases offer myriad sweet temptations, including velvety cheesecake.

Note, too, some marvelous Italian food shops here, such as tiny **Russo's Mozzarella and Pasta Corp.,** 344 East 11th St., in business since 1908 as an emporium for imported and fresh cheeses, and fresh pastas and sauce. At **Ferrucci's Gourmet Market,** around the corner at 171 First Ave., you can pick up a loaf of fresh-baked pepperoni bread, sun-dried tomatoes, and smoked mozzarella—an ambrosial sandwich combo. If you haven't eaten, Ferrucci's and Veniero's offer all you need for a tasty picnic in Tompkins Square Park (Stop 12).

Walk downtown on First Avenue toward 10th Street. Just past the southwest corner of the intersection is the:

10. **Theater for the New City (TNC).** After a quarter of a century presenting cutting-edge drama, poetry, music, dance, and the visual arts, the TNC's productions remain eclectic, politically engaged, fearless, multicultural, and creative. Go in and pick up a program or call the box office (☎ 212/254-1109) to find out what's on the program.

Cross First Avenue and walk east (take a left) onto 10th Street. On your right, at no. 268, is a venerated New York institution, the:

11. **Russian-Turkish Baths,** aka the 10th Street Baths, established in 1892 (☎ 212/674-9250). There were once numerous Turkish-style bathhouses in New York City; some of them, such as the Coney Island baths and the Luxor on 42nd Street, became the hangouts of gangsters and celebrities. In the 1970s, most New York baths became notorious yet again, this time as (often raunchy) singles' scenes for gay men. With some bordering on orgy emporiums, most of these gay baths closed their doors in the mid 1980s when AIDS became widespread and widely feared.

The Tenth Street Baths has remained staunchly straight and old-fashioned since their 19th-century inception. They are the last of the genre, open daily 9am to 10pm, with an admission of $20 (more for various special massages and

The 10th Street Baths

The regular patrons of the 10th Street Baths, who come here for a *schvitz* (Yiddish for sweat), are quite a heterogeneous group. They include Orthodox Jews, Russian wrestlers, Wall Street brokers, rap stars such as L.L. Cool J, and, on co-ed days, fashion models. John F. Kennedy Jr. has schvitzed here, as have Frank Sinatra, Mikhail Baryshnikov, and Timothy Leary. And in the early days of *Saturday Night Live,* Dan Aykroyd and John Belushi used to unwind with a postshow schvitz.

The setting is far from glamorous; the dank interior of the baths evokes a 19th-century dungeon: In the Russian Room, where 11 tons of rocks raise the temperature well above 200°F, patrons sit and steam, intermittently dumping buckets of ice water over their heads. Occasionally, they ask an attendant (in the old days a deaf-mute incapable of following the conversations of mobsters) for a *platza,* a vigorous scrubbing with a brush made of oak leaves (it opens the pores and lets toxins sweat away). Afterward, the bathers flop into an ice-cold pool, wrap themselves in robes, and head upstairs for sustenance and conversation over a meal of borscht, schmaltz herring, whitefish salad, kasha, and the like, as well as a few shots of vodka. The premises also house massage rooms (offering everything from shiatzu to Dead Sea salt rubs), a small gym, tanning, a redwood sauna, cots to lounge on, and a pine-fenced sundeck on the second floor amid treetops.

One man who has visited the baths several times a week for 75 years summed up his loyalty to the place: "When I walk out from here, I am like a newborn baby. . . . Why should I deny myself this little pleasure?"

Stop in for a look around and down a soul-warming shot of owner Boris Tuberman's homemade garlic and pepper vodka; for best results swallow it in one gulp and immediately stuff a cold pickled tomato into your mouth.

treatments; see box). Monday, Tuesday, Friday, and Saturday are co-ed, with Thursday and Sunday reserved for men only, and a ladies' day on Wednesday.

Tenth Street next intersects with the first of the "Alphabet City" thoroughfares, Avenue A. Opening up from the southeast corner of the intersection is:

12. **Tompkins Square Park.** This beautiful 16-acre park was created on a salt marsh that was known as Stuyvesant Swamp; the Stuyvesant family gave the land to the city in 1833. It is as much a focus of the East Village as Washington Square is of Greenwich Village proper. In fact, like Washington Square, it was designed to be the hub of an upscale neighborhood—a vision that never materialized due to its out-of-the-way location. While Washington Square attracts throngs of tourists, Tompkins Square remains a true neighborhood park. Many of its surrounding buildings date to the mid–19th century.

Head into the park at the 9th Street entrance. About halfway across the 9th Street walkway, through a brick portico, is an eroded monument commemorating a tragedy that was a swan song for the first immigrants to put their stamp on this area, the Germans. In 1904, the passenger ferry *General Slocum* burst into flame, was incinerated in under 15 minutes, and sank in the East River with over 1,200 aboard, most of whom were women and children from the East Village's "Dutchtown" ("Dutch" is a common corruption of Deutsch—German for "German"). The aging ship hadn't updated its safety equipment in years. The undrilled crew hefted the dried old canvas fire hoses, but the useless things burst under the water pressure; frightened passengers grabbed rotted life preservers, which crumbled to dust in their hands. Many of the survivors, who lost friends and even entire families, found it emotionally impossible to continue living here after the disaster and moved to other German neighborhoods in the city. As Germans moved uptown, Eastern European Jews moved in.

Follow the park's walkways toward the southwest and, just behind the playground, you'll see the Temperance Fountain under a classical stone canopy, built in 1888 in hopes of convincing the thirsty to choose water over alcoholic spirits.

At the southwest corner of the park is a statue of Congressman Samuel Cox, the "Postman's Friend," whose efforts to increase salaries and improve working conditions in the U.S. Postal Service made him a sort of patron saint of letter carriers.

Over the years, Tompkins Square has frequently been the site of riots and rebellions. In the 19th and early 20th centuries, it functioned as a venue for socialist and labor rallies. In 1874, one such gathering, resulting from a financial panic, was violently dispersed by city police, an event that became known as the Tompkins Square Massacre. Numerous peace rallies—not to mention some great rock concerts—took place here during the Vietnam War era.

Tensions in recent years, arising from the real estate industry's attempts to gentrify the neighborhood, have focused on the Christadora House (at the northeast corner of Ninth Street and Avenue B), converted to high-priced condominiums by developers in 1987. It became the target of antigentrification forces when, in 1988, police attempted to enforce a curfew in the park and an ugly riot ensued. Officers clubbed and arrested not only protesters but innocent bystanders, and vandals did extensive damage to the Christadora. In the 1990s, the park has been extensively renovated and an encampment of homeless people was forced to move elsewhere, although by day, they still make it their living room.

These tumultuous events notwithstanding, the park is essentially a recreational setting: Children entertain themselves in playgrounds, fierce hoop action enlivens the basketball courts, swimmers cool off in the pool (open every summer), and people sunbathe on expanses of lawn and picnic under ancient elms.

Leave the park on the Avenue A side (north) and stroll west toward First Avenue along St. Marks Place, which is lined with neighborhood cafes, thrift shops, and tattoo parlors. Just across First Avenue on the north side of the street is:

13. **W.H. Auden's home,** at 77 St. Marks Place. Auden lived and worked in a third-floor apartment here, amid a clutter of books and manuscripts, from 1953 to 1972, a year before his death. Although he generally kept a low profile in the neighborhood, he occasionally breakfasted on scotch at the Holiday Cocktail Lounge next door (no. 75), and was a parishioner at St. Mark's-in-the-Bowery. Earlier in the century, the Russian Communist periodical *Novy Mir* was published at no. 77. Leon Trotsky, a contributor, came by when he visited New York in 1917.

Across the street is:

14. **Theatre 80 St. Marks.** Until the advent of VCRs, revival cinema houses flourished in New York. This 160-seat facility was one of the last of the genre. It opened originally as a live theater in 1967; its first show, *You're a Good Man Charlie Brown,* played to sellout audiences for 4½ years. From 1971 on, proprietor Howard Otway, a former stage actor, dreamt up appealing double features and made his theater a shrine to the silver screen, adorned with photographs of the matinee idols of yesteryear. After Otway died in 1993, his son Lawrence decided to use the space for theatrical productions once more.

   Today, 80 St. Marks is the home of a classical repertory group called the Pearl Theatre Company (☎ **212/ 596-9802**), which for 10 years was located in Chelsea. Unlike many contemporary theater companies, the Pearl does traditional interpretations of classic plays.

   Keep following this street west and you will soon reach the surreal center of the East Village counterculture:

15. **St. Marks Place,** between Second and Third avenues. Today populated by punks, anarchists, and various street people who defy categorization, this hippie mecca of the 1960s and 1970s has declined to a state of general seediness. Adding insult to injury, it has been besmirched by a branch of the Gap, an advent as astonishing in the East Village as the appearance of McDonald's on Paris' Champs-Elysées. One landmark of days gone by is the Gem Spa, at the corner of Second Avenue, ever and always the area's most famous egg cream venue. Funky shops along the street sell cheap jewelry, alt-rock T-shirts, leather, and tapes and CDs, augmented, unless there has recently been a bust, by peddlers hawking used books and incense.

   On the north side of the block, the bright blue building occupying nos. 19 through 25 is the:

16. **All-Craft Foundation,** an organization that helps homeless and drug-addicted people in the community. However, the building was once home to the Electric Circus, the disco that succeeded Andy Warhol's Exploding Plastic Inevitable (a multimedia event combining his films with live music, dancing, light show effects, and bizarre live action) at a bar

called the Dom below. Before that, it was called Arlington Hall, a ballroom rented out mainly for neighborhood weddings, bar mitzvahs, and other celebrations.

There were also a few gangster "rackets" held at Arlington, the most famous in January 9, 1914, when Italian mobster Jack Sirocco had the nerve to throw a ball here—in the middle of a Jewish gang-controlled neighborhood, and right in the midst of a turf war with neighborhood chief hood, Dopey Benny Fein. Fein was an "honorable thief" of sorts who controlled unions and played tough on the side of laborers against corrupt management. Sirocco, on the other hand, had his fingers deep in the capitalist pie. Just 2 months before the big "racket", Sirocco's outfit banged heads with Fein's gang—defending management's side in a strike, one of Sirocco's goons offed a Fein flunky. As Sirocco's thugs climbed the stairs to the party on January 9, Fein's boys, loitering in the doorways across the street, opened fire and plastered the Arlington's walls with a spray of bullets. Sirocco's men returned fire. Surprisingly abysmal shots on both sides, the gangsters collectively succeeded in hitting, and killing, only an innocent bystander. No one was ever convicted, but Fein's power was effectively broken. Several years later, Dopey Benny Fein quietly squealed to the DA, and then went straight.

Make your way back to Second Avenue and turn right, then turn right again onto 7th Street. On the north side of the street, at no. 31, look for the granite facade into which is carved the name of the:

17. **Hebrew Actors Union.** During the heyday of Yiddish theater on Second Avenue, even the biggest stars used to pay regular visits to this building. Today, despite the almost total demise of the Jewish Rialto, the union is still active.

Further along 7th Street is one of the few vestiges of the days when the East Village had a significant Irish population:

18. **McSorley's Old Ale House and Grill,** 15 East 7th St. (☎ 212/473-9148), one of New York's oldest watering holes, established in 1854. It looks (and smells) every bit its age. The wood floor is strewn with sawdust, and the pressed-tin walls are cluttered with a thicket of photos and newspaper clippings, all gone yellow with age and a century's worth

of tobacco smoke, interspersed among an odd assortment of knickknacks and mementos.

Over the years, luminaries from Peter Cooper to Brendan Behan have earned the right to a particular chair or bar stool, and the bar's beery charm was captured in Joseph Mitchell's *New Yorker* stories, later collected in a book, *McSorley's Wonderful Saloon.* Artist John Sloan immortalized the saloon's unique atmosphere in a painting called *A Mug of Ale at McSorley's* (1913). Perhaps the only significant change McSorley's has undergone this century was to open its doors to women in 1971. If you drop in on an afternoon for a mug of sweet McSorley's ale (the food here, deli sandwiches and chili, is not notable), you'll catch a glimpse of the New York Peter Cooper knew.

These days, 7th Street is the heart of a Ukrainian immigrant community some 20,000 strong. Representative of this is:

19. **Surma,** a store-cum-community center at no. 11, selling Ukrainian newspapers and books and Eastern European handicrafts. The latter include embroidered peasant blouses (Karen Allen wore one in the film *Raiders of the Lost Ark),* paintings, traditional porcelain, dolls, and *pysanky* (decorated eggs; see Stop 9). Across the street is **St. George's Ukrainian Catholic Church,** its dome adorned with 16 beautiful stained-glass windows.

Across Third Avenue from 7th Street is:

20. **Cooper Square.** Situated on this wedge-shaped lot are the chocolate-brown Cooper Union Foundation Building and a small park housing a bronze likeness of Peter Cooper (1791–1883)—inventor, industrialist, philanthropist, and one of the great geniuses of his day. He made the bulk of his fortune through an ironworks and a glue factory, built the first steam locomotive in the United States (the *Tom Thumb*), developed the first rolled-steel railroad rails, and was instrumental in laying the first transatlantic telegraph cable. Cooper, a self-educated man from modest roots, believed that his wealth carried with it a responsibility to improve the working man's situation, and so he founded the Cooper Union to provide free education in the practical trades and arts to any man or woman who wished to attend. A sense of Cooper as a benevolent, fatherly figure

flows from the statue, and it's only natural: The sculptor, Augustus Saint-Gaudens, was able to attend Cooper Union's art school because of its founder's characteristic generosity.

The Cooper Union Foundation Building was completed in 1859. It was the first building in New York to use wrought-iron beams (another Cooper innovation), the forerunners of the steel I-beams that are the skeleton of present-day skyscrapers. The Italianate brownstone exterior remains much as it was in the 19th century. The interior, however, underwent extensive renovations in 1975.

From the lobby, you can see an elaborate and amusing carved-wood birthday card on the back wall, given to the founder by the senior class of 1871 to thank him for his 80th birthday gift of $150,000 to the school. To get past the security desk and down the stairs to the Great Hall (below), you must get permission from the Public Affairs office on the 8th floor of **30 Cooper Square**. In keeping with Peter Cooper's designs for it, the Great Hall has functioned over the years as a free public forum in which great issues of the day are debated. Labor leader Samuel Gompers, free-love advocate Victoria Woodhull, and Sioux chief Red Cloud all spoke here, but perhaps the Great Hall's most famous moment occurred in 1860, when Abraham Lincoln's fiery "right makes might" antislavery speech carried public opinion in New York and sped him to the Republican Party's presidential nomination.

Also on Cooper Square are the offices of New York's most popular liberal rag and events mag, *The Village Voice*.

Walk around Cooper Union, turn left on Astor Place, then hang another left onto Lafayette Street. A few paces down on your left is the:

21. **Joseph Papp Public Theater.** The Public, one of New York's most vital cultural institutions, is housed in the old Astor Library. This redbrick German Romanesque–Revival–style palace, the first public library in the United States, was the lone public bequest of John Jacob Astor, who made millions in the fur trade and was a notoriously tightfisted landowner. In 1911 the library's collection was moved to the New York Public Library on 42nd Street. From 1920 to 1966, the Hebrew Immigrant Aid Society used the building to shelter and feed thousands of Jewish immigrants

and help them gain a footing in the United States. When they moved out, city officials and Joseph Papp's New York Shakespeare Festival rescued the Astor Library from a developer who had planned to raze it to make way for an apartment complex; the building was designated a city landmark and became the permanent indoor home of the New York Shakespeare Festival.

The Public Theater opened in 1967 with the original production of *Hair,* which moved on to Broadway; in 1975 *A Chorus Line* followed suit, becoming one of the longest-running shows in Broadway history. Over the years, the New York Shakespeare Festival has presented on the Public's five stages new plays by such major playwrights as David Rabe, John Guare, David Mamet, Caryl Churchill, Sam Shepard, and Larry Kramer. Joseph Papp died in 1992, but the theater continues to thrive, with cinema offerings, poetry readings, lectures, a cafe, a bookstore, and a late-night cabaret added to the offerings. Unsold theater tickets are often available as half-price "Quiktix" after 6pm (1pm for matinees on Saturday and Sunday) in the lobby.

Across the street from the Public Theater is:

22. **Colonnade Row,** a group of row houses fronted by a crumbling marble colonnade. Of the nine row houses built by developer Seth Geer in 1831, only four remain; the five on the south end were demolished to make room for the Wanamaker Department Store warehouse. Lafayette Street was once a quiet, posh residential district. John Jacob Astor lived here, as did members of the Vanderbilt and Delano families and writer Washington Irving. President John Tyler married Franklin Delano's daughter, Julia, here in 1844. The fashionable set moved uptown after the Civil War and these houses have been in decline ever since.

Turn back and walk toward Astor Place. The black metal sculpture that dominates the traffic island in the middle of the intersection is the:

23. **"Alamo,"** known universally to area residents as "the Cube." Sculptor Tony Rosenthal built the piece in 1967 for a city-sponsored exhibition. He is reportedly pleased that the "Alamo" has become a participatory piece—it was built on a rotating post so that it could be positioned after

installation, but it has become a tradition in the East Village for anyone feeling a bit rowdy to spin the Cube.

The next and last stop is on the adjoining traffic island across 8th Street, the:

24. **Astor Place subway kiosk.** Earlier in this century, almost every IRT subway stop in Manhattan had a kiosk much like this one. The Transit Authority inexplicably decided to tear them all down in 1911, but when the Astor Place subway station was restored in 1985, officials revived what had been a lost element of New York City's architectural scene. (Down in the station, Milton Glaser's mosaics and the ceramic low-relief tiles depicting beavers—the animal whose pelt made John Jacob Astor's fortune—are worth a look.) Peter Cooper would no doubt have been deeply satisfied to know that the architect of the new kiosk was a Cooper Union graduate.

Midtown

Start: Grand Central Terminal.

Subway: Take the 4, 5, 6, 7, or the shuttle to 42nd Street/ Grand Central.

Finish: The Plaza Hotel.

Time: Approximately 4 hours, not counting time for browsing in shops and galleries.

Best Time: Weekdays, when Midtown is bustling but the attractions aren't packed as they tend to be on weekends.

Worst Time: Rush hour (weekdays from 8:30 to 9:30am and from 4:30 to 6pm).

If there's an area that defines New York in the popular imagination, it's Midtown. Concentrated here are dozens of the towering skyscrapers that are so closely identified with the city and its skyline. Lining Fifth Avenue and 57th Street are blue-chip art galleries, high-toned boutiques, chic department stores, and, increasingly, theme restaurants like Hard Rock Cafe that make New York the consumer capital of the world. Midtown is Manhattan at its most glamorous.

• • • • • • • • • • • • • • •

Midtown

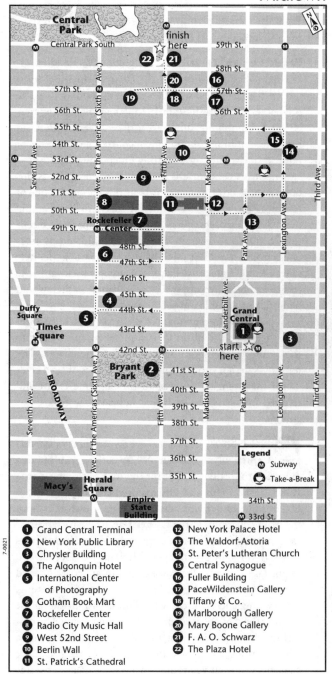

1. Grand Central Terminal
2. New York Public Library
3. Chrysler Building
4. The Algonquin Hotel
5. International Center of Photography
6. Gotham Book Mart
7. Rockefeller Center
8. Radio City Music Hall
9. West 52nd Street
10. Berlin Wall
11. St. Patrick's Cathedral
12. New York Palace Hotel
13. The Waldorf-Astoria
14. St. Peter's Lutheran Church
15. Central Synagogue
16. Fuller Building
17. PaceWildenstein Gallery
18. Tiffany & Co.
19. Marlborough Gallery
20. Mary Boone Gallery
21. F. A. O. Schwarz
22. The Plaza Hotel

115

From the subway platform, follow the Metro North signs to the main concours of:

1. **Grand Central Terminal.** Commodore Vanderbilt himself named the station "Grand Central" in the 1860s, despite the fact that it was then out in the boondocks. The present terminal was built in 1913. It's an engineering tour de force, combining subways, surface streets, pedestrian malls, underground shopping concourses, and 48 pairs of railroad tracks into one smoothly functioning organism.

   The main concourse is breathtaking, emerging as this book goes to print from a multiyear restoration. It's one of America's most impressive interior spaces, with gleaming marble floors, sweeping staircases, and an aqua vaulted ceiling soaring 125 feet high. Twenty-five hundred pinpricks of electronic stars litter this "sky" with a view of a Mediterranean winter sky's constellations (seemingly backwards, the zodiac symbols are supposedly represented as they would be seen from outside our solar system).

   When a developer announced plans to place a huge tower over the concourse in the 1970s, preservationists came to the rescue, with Jackie Onassis leading the charge. The terminal's design survived intact after a series of legal challenges that went all the way to the Supreme Court and resulted in a 1978 decision that upheld New York City's landmarks laws.

   Take a Break There are numerous spots in Grand Central where you can pick up coffee, a muffin, or a sandwich to fortify yourself for the tour, including **Zaro's Bread Basket, Hot and Crusty,** or **Häagen-Dazs.**

   For something more substantial, head downstairs from the main concourse to the **Oyster Bar,** where passable seafood is served in a first-rate setting of wide-vaulted ceilings Monday through Friday from 11:30am to 9:30pm. You might take a seat at the counter for an appetizer of fried oysters, New Zealand greenlip mussels in Dijon dressing, or New England clam chowder. Full meals, including the catch of the day, are available in the dining room. The dessert menu features key lime pie and bread pudding, and a wine bar offers a large selection of wines by the glass. The acoustics of the curved ceiling "whispering gallery" outside the restaurant's entrance allows people to stand in opposite corners and hold a whispered conversation.

Leave the main concourse via the 42nd Street exit and turn right. Walk west for two blocks and then make a left onto Fifth Avenue, where the:

2. **New York Public Library** sits in splendor, resembling a Greek temple with rows of Corinthian columns. Completed in 1911, this beaux arts palace, one of the greatest research libraries in the world, cost $10 million to construct, and President Taft himself attended the dedication ceremony. Everything inside was designed as a unit, from the marble walls to the chairs, stepladders, and wastebaskets.

Climb up the broad stone steps guarded by twin stone lions, named *Patience* and *Fortitude* by mayor Fiorello LaGuardia in the 1930s—the qualities he proclaimed New Yorkers would need to survive the depression. Cafes on either side of the grounds, past fountains marked by classical statuary, offer umbrella tables.

It's well worth exploring the interior, which contains manuscripts, maps, journals, prints, and more than 38 million volumes occupying 80 miles of bookshelves. There's an information desk just inside the lobby, which is made entirely of unmortared Vermont marble, where you can sign up for tours (offered at 11am and 2pm). The staff can point you to the library's current exhibits, its wonderful bookstore and gift shop, and to the third-floor main reading room, a magnificent space extending the entire block-long length of the building. In July 1997, the library started a renovation scheduled to last at least 18 months that will close various rooms in turn. The library is open Monday and Thursday through Saturday 10am to 6pm; Tuesday and Wednesday 11am to 7:30pm.

Turn left out of the library to head uptown on the west side of Fifth Avenue. Look up and to your right as you cross 42nd Street to get a wonderful perspective view down the block to the:

3. **Chrysler Building.** At 1,046 feet, this art deco masterpiece reigned briefly in 1930 as the tallest building in the world until the Empire State Building came along. The stainless steel spire with its thrusting gargoyles creates one of the

most beautiful and distinctive features of the Manhattan skyline.

Continue north on Fifth Avenue for two blocks to 44th Street, where you'll turn left. On the north side of 44th, at no. 27, is the **Harvard Club,** designed by McKim, Mead, and White in 1894 in an architectural style that was favored at Harvard in the 1800s. The "Veritas" coat of arms tops the building. A few doors down at no. 37 is the **Yacht Club,** with a fanciful and flowing concrete facade.

Continue along 44th Street. Near Sixth Avenue stands one of New York's most famous literary landmarks:

4. **The Algonquin Hotel.** H.L. Mencken, a Baltimore resident, began staying at the Algonquin on his frequent business trips to New York after he became the editor of *Smart Set* in 1914. Under Mencken's stewardship, the magazine published the early works of Eugene O'Neill, James Joyce, and F. Scott Fitzgerald. Nonetheless, Mencken detested the city and remained unimpressed by its young bohemian writers ("The Village literati are scum," he pronounced).

As *Smart Set* faded from influence in the 1920s, *Vanity Fair* began to take its place, counting Edna St. Vincent Millay, Elinor Wylie, and Theodore Dreiser among its contributors. In its offices at 19 West 44th St., Dorothy Parker, Robert Benchley, and Robert Sherwood served on the editorial staff. They began hanging out in the Algonquin, and soon their gatherings grew into the famous "Round Table," which also included Alexander Woolcott (drama critic for *The New York Times*), George S. Kaufman, Franklin Adams (columnist for the *New York World*), and Edna Ferber. The group became famous for its witty, acerbic commentary on theater, literature, and the social scene, though Dorothy Parker herself played down its importance: "The Round Table was just a lot of people telling jokes and telling each other how good they were."

One of the regulars, Harold Ross, took it into his head to start a magazine that would incorporate the group's sophisticated, satirical outlook, and rounded up investors to begin publication of *The New Yorker,* with offices set up nearby at 25 West 45th St. The first few issues were extremely uneven, but within a couple of years E.B. White and James Thurber had been added to the staff and were reshaping the magazine into one of the most prestigious publications in the country.

Even after the Round Table stopped gathering at the hotel, the Algonquin continued to count famous writers among its guests, including Gertude Stein and her companion Alice B. Toklas, F. Scott Fitzgerald, and William Faulkner, who wrote the acceptance speech for his 1949 Nobel Prize on Algonquin stationery.

To further soak up this hotel's genteel ambience, consider having lunch or weekend brunch in the Rose Room. Or ensconce yourself with a cocktail in a comfortable sofa of the lobby lounge, where *New Yorker* writers frequently conduct interviews.

Across the street from the Algonquin, but light-years away in design, is the **Royalton Hotel.** Poke your head inside and take a look—the whimsically futuristic "Jetsons"-style decor, created by Philippe Starck, has to be seen to be believed.

Cross Sixth Avenue (aka Avenue of the Americas) and turn left. Before the corner of 43rd Street is the midtown branch of the:

5. **International Center of Photography** (☎ 212/768-4680), which presents around 30 photography shows annually, open Tuesday 11am to 8pm and Wednesday through Sunday 11am to 6pm. Celebrating various trends, artists, and themes, these are some of the best photo shows in the city, well worth the low admission charge. They also run expensive but well-regarded courses in the craft.

Double back north along Sixth Avenue to 47th Street, where you'll take a right. This block, between Fifth and Sixth Avenues, is the **Diamond District,** where millions of dollars' worth of gems are traded every day. The business hustle on this block makes an unlikely setting for another literary sight, the:

6. **Gotham Book Mart** (☎ 212/719-4448), on the north side at no. 41. Originally founded in 1920 on West 45th Street, the store moved here in 1923. H.L. Mencken and his friend Theodore Dreiser once stopped in, and, delighted to find some of their own works in stock, began to scribble dedications on many of the books, including the Bible, which they signed "With the compliments of the authors."

The store has hosted countless book publication parties, and the list of writers toasted here has included Dylan Thomas, Katherine Anne Porter, William Carlos Williams, W.H. Auden, Marianne Moore, Joyce Carol Oates, and Tennessee Williams. The most famous such gathering was the 1939 "wake" held to celebrate the publication of James Joyce's *Finnegans Wake*. In 1947, the store became headquarters of the James Joyce Society, whose first membership was purchased by T.S. Eliot.

Owner Frances Steloff (who died in 1989 at the age of 101) was known for lending a hand to perennially cash-strapped artists such as Henry Miller and John Dos Passos (even Martha Graham borrowed $1,000 to stage her first dance performance). This tradition grew into the Writers' Emergency Fund, which still offers loans to struggling scribes.

Turn left up Fifth Avenue to 49th Street. On the right side of the Avenue stands one of New York's most famous department stores, **Saks Fifth Avenue.** Immediately opposite Saks, head west into the promenade of:

7. **Rockefeller Center,** one of the most handsome urban complexes in New York. It encompasses 24 acres and 19 skyscrapers, extending from 47th to 52nd streets between Fifth and Sixth avenues. People scoffed at John D. Rockefeller in 1929 when he unveiled plans to build this "city within a city," since it was so far removed from what was then the commercial heart of New York. But Rockefeller proved all the critics wrong. His complex remade the map, drawing business uptown and setting the standard for future civic projects by incorporating public art and open spaces.

Stroll west through the Channel Gardens to Rockefeller Center's famous skating rink. In the summer, this area becomes an outdoor cafe; in cooler months, it's packed with skaters gliding along the ice to music and the twinkle of tiny lights in the trees. Each holiday season a giant Christmas tree stands here, towering over the promenade. Paul Manship's massive *Prometheus* lounges above the skating rink, beneath a quote from Aeschylus.

Take a look inside the lobby of 30 Rockefeller Plaza, once the RCA Building and now renamed the GE Building. Above the black marble floors and walls are monumental sepia-toned murals by José Maria Sert. This art deco building was featured in the movie *Quiz Show*.

Just to the left of 30 Rockefeller Plaza, head west (right) on 49th Street to Sixth Avenue. You'll pass the wrap-around corner windows with a digital news feed where early risers peer through the glass and wave in the hopes of becoming part of the backdrop during filming of NBC's *Today* show just inside.

When you reach Sixth Avenue, turn right and head uptown. A building boom in the 1960s and 1970s transformed this area into a canyon of 50-story glass skyscrapers. Although the buildings individually aren't of great note, together they form an urban environment of considerable grandeur.

On the right side of Sixth Avenue, north of 50th Street, stands:

8. **Radio City Music Hall** has been restored to its 1930s art deco elegance. Its original owner, Samuel "Roxy" Rothafel, ran it as a vaudeville house, but the enterprise was a flop and Rothafel sold out to the Rockefellers. Today shows here run the gamut from performances by headliners such as Liza Minelli to the annual Christmas Spectacular, starring Radio City's own Rockettes and a cast that includes live animals (picture camels sauntering in through the Sixth Avenue entrance). Hour-long guided tours are offered every half-hour daily from 10am to 5pm; call ☎ 212/ 632-4941 for information, and buy tickets in the gift shop to the left of the entrance.

Continue up Sixth Avenue and take a right on

9. **West 52nd Street,** designated "Swing Street" since this block holds a special place in jazz history. It was lined with a number of illicit speakeasies during Prohibition, and after its repeal, many of the establishments became jazz clubs, nurturing such great talents as Billie Holliday, Fats Waller, Dizzy Gillespie, Charlie Parker, and Sarah Vaughan.

The **Twenty-one Club,** at 21 West 52nd St. (☎ 212/ 582-7200), is still a popular restaurant and one of the few establishments to survive from this era. Operating as a speakeasy during Prohibition, it relied on several clever devices to guard against police raids, including a trap door on the bar that sent everyone's cocktails tumbling into the sewer when a button was pressed. Today it serves excellent food in a tavern atmosphere—if you can get a reservation in the popular dining room. The front "smoking room" is open to anyone who wanders in. The club is closed weekends in summer and Sundays year-round.

Across the street, inside the lobby of the office building at no. 22, is **Traveller's Bookstore,** a small store with a knowledgeable staff selling nothing but travel guides and related literature.

Continue down 52nd Street. Near the end of the block, take a left under the modern passageway, numbered 666 Fifth Avenue, through to 53rd Street. Under here, you'll pass by an undulating stainless steel wall **waterfall** designed by Isamu Noguchi. When you pop out onto 53rd Street, you'll be turning right to continue the tour. However, museum shop aficionados can hang a left and jog half a block down to the **Museum of Modern Art's (MoMA) bookshop** and, the design store across the street.

Turning right onto 53rd Street, cross Fifth Avenue and walk two-thirds of 53rd's next block to the second small granite-and-waterfall, pocket-sized park, where sits a brief, graffiti-covered stretch of the:

10. **Berlin Wall.** Return to Fifth Avenue and take a left to cruise past glitzy outposts of high fashion, including Ferragamo, Cartier, and Versace. Between 51st and 50th streets rises the unmistakable neo-Gothic bulk of:

11. **St. Patrick's Cathedral,** the seat of the Archdiocese of New York and largest Catholic cathedral in America. Designed by James Renwick in 1858 and modeled after Cologne's cathedral, it's a magnificent structure, with twin spires rising 330 feet above street level. Construction took 21 years. Zelda and F. Scott Fitzgerald were married here in 1920.

Across the street as you exit, in front of 630 Fifth Ave., crouches Lee Lawrie's 1937 *Atlas,* one of New York's most famous statues in 15 feet of bronze.

Walk along the north (left) side of the church on 51st Street. Cross Madison Avenue and take a right down it, admiring the Gothic-style tracery on the backside of St.

Paddy's across the street. On your left, the block is filled with the brownstone-gone-amok mass of the:

12. **New York Palace Hotel,** Also known as the Villard Houses after the Bavarian immigrant Henry Villard, who published the *New York Evening Post* and founded the Northern Pacific Railroad. He commissioned the unified buildings from McKim, Mead, and White in 1881. Today it's home to one of New York's most oft-reinvented and posh restaurants, **Le Cirque 2000**(☎ 212/303-7712); the **Urban Center** (☎ 212/935-3592), whose bookshop is a treasure trove of tomes on architecture; and, in the hotel itself through the central doors, a compact architectural fantasyland of gilt, marble, sweeping staircases, crystal chandeliers, and opulent meeting rooms.

Take a left onto 50th Street and walk toward Park Avenue. As you look right down Park, you'll see the **Helmsley Building,** a lovely structure that sits astride the Avenue, crowned with an elaborate cupola. The building is overshadowed by the Met Life building, one of New York's greatest architectural travesties.

Across Park Avenue, between 50th and 49th Streets, stands one of the most famous hotels in the world:

13. **The Waldorf-Astoria.** For almost a century, the Waldorf has been synonymous with wealth and luxury. In 1897, in the midst of a devastating economic depression, society matron Mrs. Bradley Martin decided to hold a costume ball here for 1,200 guests, who were to attend dressed in the style of the court of Versailles. When details of the preparations, rumored to top a quarter of a million dollars, hit the papers, outrage ran high. A huge squad of police officers, personally supervised by police commissioner Teddy Roosevelt (whose wife was inside enjoying the festivities), had to be positioned around the hotel to prevent the great unwashed from venting their resentment.

Cole Porter and his wife lived here for many years in one of the permanent apartments in the Waldorf Towers; one of the hotel's dining spots, Peacock Alley, still boasts his piano. Other famous residents have included Gen. Douglas MacArthur, Herbert Hoover, Henry and Clare Booth Luce, and the Duke and Duchess of Windsor. Gangster

Lucky Luciano also lived here under an alias until he was forced to leave the Waldorf for less luxurious digs—in the state penitentiary.

Between 50th and 51st streets on Park Avenue lies **St. Bartholomew's,** a domed Episcopal church sporting a Byzantine style that seems startling in this location.

☕ **Take a Break**   St. Bart's may be the only church in New York with its own terrace cafe—**Café St. Bart's** (☎ **212/935-8434**). Under large umbrellas, with the Byzantine building shading you, you can dine al fresco on scrumptious salads (chicken curry with apples and walnuts is good) and sandwiches—try the Chelsea, smoked turkey, brie, honey mustard, and endive on a baguette. Salads and sandwiches run $6.25 to $9.75, with pasta dishes and steaks a bit more. In summer, the terrace presents live music; in winter, the cafe moves indoors into an uninspired back room of the church's complex.

Walk around the left side of St. Bart's down 51st Street to Lexington Avenue and turn left up the east side of it. The subway grating on this block is perhaps the most famous in the world, ever since 1955 when one of its gusts of hot air sent the skirt of Marilyn Monroe's dress billowing right into pin-up legend in *The Seven Year Itch.*

Continue north up Lexington to 53rd Street, where the corner office building (no. 599 Lexington) features Frank Stella's *Salto nel Mio Sacco,* a colorful 1985 work, in the lobby. Across 53rd Street from this is the austere, glass-and-buffed-aluminum pinnacle of **Citicorp Center.** This pillar of international finance incorporates, at the corner of 54th Street, the modern and angular:

14. **St. Peter's Lutheran Church,** built in 1977 and a singularly hip house of worship. Adorned with sculpture by Louise Nevelson (check out the Erol Baeker Chapel of the Good Shepard), St. Peter's is famous for its Sunday evening Jazz Vespers, where many of the greatest names in jazz have performed. Besides the permanent Nevelson sculptures and a Pomodoro *Cross* out front, St. Peter's also regularly displays works by contemporary artists.

    Just north of St. Peter's, at 55th Street and across Lexington, is the:

15. **Central Synagogue,** one of New York's finest examples of Moorish-Revival–style architecture. The oldest synagogue in continuous use in the city, it was dedicated in 1870. It's only open noon to 2pm, Monday through Thursday.

    Turn left on 55th Street and right on Park Avenue. On your left, you'll pass a **Mercedes showroom**—the curvilinear interior was designed by Frank Lloyd Wright long before he conceived of his more famous New York landmark, the Guggenheim.

    Fifty-seventh Street is home to many of the city's top art galleries and upscale boutiques. From Park Avenue turn left along it, and you'll come to the beautiful black-and-white art deco:

16. **Fuller Building** at the northeast corner of Madison Avenue and 57th Street. Look at the bronze doors, the marble fixtures, and mosaic floors—and plan to spend some time browsing in the many art galleries housed here. Try to hit **Andre Emmerich,** a division of Sotheby's whose list of major contemporary artists includes Josef Albers, Keith Haring, David Hockney, Hans Hofmann, and Jules Olitski. **Robert Miller** shows modern painting and photography from the likes of Louise Fishman, Eva Hesse, Robert Mapplethorpe, Joan Mitchell, Alice Neel, and Philip Pearstein. Also of interest is **George Adams** (7th floor), which has been here for 30 years and features ceramicist Robert Arneson, Realists Jack Beal and Alfred Leslie, and the colorfully eccentric paintings of Peter Saul.

    Across 57th Street at no. 40 is:

17. **PaceWildenstein Gallery,** a major art gallery with specialty dealers spread out on several floors. The main gallery is devoted to 20th-century painting, drawing, and sculpture. It shows blue chip artists like Georg Baselitz, Alexander Calder, Chuck Close, Jim Dine, Jean Dubuffet, Agnes Martin, Louise Nevelson, Isamu Noguchi, Pablo Picasso, Mark Rothko, Julian Schnabel, and Richard Serra. On the 10th floor are **Pace Primitive Art** (African and Asian art) and **Pace Master Prints and Drawings** (prints and drawings by old masters like Durer, Goya, Matisse, Picasso, Piranesi, Rembrandt, and Whistler). On the third floor are **PaceWildensteinMacGill** (20th-century photography) and

Pace Prints, which carries contemporary prints by many of the same artists that show in the main gallery.

Continue along 57th Street to Fifth Avenue. On your left stretches the bejeweled:

18. **Tiffany & Co.,** with its windows full of amazing gems. Audrey Hepburn gracefully strolled by here as Holly Golightly in *Breakfast at Tiffany's.*

    Cross Fifth Avenue and continue along West 57th Street. Halfway down the next block, at no. 40, on your left is the:

19. **Marlborough Gallery** (second floor), one of the most reputable galleries in the world, whose big stars include the late Francis Bacon (Britain's de Kooning), Fernando Botero, Red Grooms, Alex Katz, Antonio Lopez Garcia, Tom Otterness, and Larry Rivers.

    Return to Fifth Avenue, cross it again, and turn left (uptown) up it, passing some of the city's most glamorous shops. On the east (right) side of the street at no. 745, you'll find:

20. **Mary Boone Gallery** (fourth floor), a world-class gallery of contemporary art by Richard Artschwager, Ross Bleckner, Eric Fischl, Sean Scully, and Tim Rollins and K.O.S. (Rollins worked with street kids and, in an effort to control and engage them, started them on art projects, sold to benefit the outreach program. The unlikely team became very influential in the '80s art world.) Also in this building is the **McKee Gallery**, which shows Philip Guston, a major abstract expressionist; also shown here are Jake Berthot, David Humphrey, Martin Puryear, and Jeanne Silverthrone.

    Continue up Fifth Avenue, pausing to take a peek at the wildly creative design inside the Warner Brothers store. Just north of 58th Street is the toy store of every child's dreams:

21. **F.A.O. Schwarz.** You may remember Tom Hanks's famous dance interpretation of "Heart and Soul," performed here on a giant piano keyboard in the movie *Big.* The store is a wonderland of toys, with a menagerie of stuffed animals; fantastic, mobile Lego creations; squadrons of Barbie dolls; a candy shop; and command centers of video games where anybody can play.

    Across from F.A.O. Schwarz stands the landmark:

22. **The Plaza Hotel,** built in 1907. Back then, suites rented for $25 a night. Zelda Fitzgerald turned heads here by making a splash (literally) in the fountain in front of the hotel. The Fitzgeralds stayed here in September 1922 while looking for a home, and F. Scott used the Plaza as the backdrop for a crucial scene in his masterpiece, *The Great Gatsby.* Another famous guest, Frank Lloyd Wright, stayed in a suite overlooking the park while he designed the Guggenheim Museum. Young visitors will be familiar with the Plaza as the heroine's home in the children's classic *Eloise,* movie buffs will recognize it from *Crocodile Dundee, The Cotton Club, North by Northwest, Network, Arthur, Home Alone 2,* and, of course, *Plaza Suite. Little known trivia:* 1920s Plaza chef Hector Boiardi decided to bottle his Italian pasta-and-sauce dishes for the masses—on the labels he phoneticized his name to Boy-ar-dee.

Head back downtown on Fifth Avenue.

Winding Down There's no better place to stop for an afternoon cocktail than the bar where the Bloody Mary was invented—the **King Cole Bar and Lounge,** in the St. Regis Hotel, 2 East 55th St., adorned with a wonderful mural of the old monarch himself. There's also an elegant afternoon tea served in the Astor Court, a plush venue with a vaulted ceiling, trompe l'oeil cloud murals, and exquisite 22-karat gold leafing.

The hotel itself is a landmark, built in 1904 by John Jacob Astor and housing some of the most expensive rooms in the city. Ernest Hemingway, Alfred Hitchcock, and Salvador Dalí all stayed at the St. Regis, and John Lennon and Yoko Ono occupied suites here in the early 1970s.

Central Park

Start: Grand Army Plaza, at 59th Street and Fifth Avenue.

Subway: Take the N or R to Fifth Avenue.

Finish: The Vanderbilt Gate, the entrance to the Conservatory Garden, at 105th Street and Fifth Avenue.

Time: Approximately 5 hours, including lunch. If you want to explore more fully (stopping to visit the zoo for an hour or two, for instance), consider breaking up this tour into a 2-day excursion.

Best Time: Weekends, weather permitting, when the park hums with activity.

Central Park was designed by landscape architects par excellence Frederick Law Olmsted and Calvert Vaux in the late 1850s, when its land was still on the outskirts of the city. Its advent ensured that New Yorkers would always have recourse to pastoral tranquillity. One of the world's most beautiful urban parks, it's a recreational greenbelt of woodlands, wisteria-shaded arbors, duck- and swan-filled lakes and lagoons, meadows, rambling lanes, gardens, fountains, pavilions, and picturesque bridges. Encompassing 843 acres enclosed by stone walls, the park is 2½ miles long (extending from 59th to 110th streets) and a half mile wide (from Fifth Avenue to Central Park West). It's the scene of numerous concerts, theatrical productions, and events ranging from jogging marathons to bird-watching walks. There are playing fields for sports, bridal trails, biking paths, boating lakes, a lovely zoo, gardens, playgrounds, and dozens of statues dotting the park. On weekends especially, musicians, acrobats, puppeteers, and other enterprising performers offer a wealth of free entertainment. The Central Park Conservancy and the NYC Parks Department have renovated more than a third of Central Park over the past decade, and the park today is safe, clean, and beautiful.

• • • • • • • • • • • • • • • •

Consider starting out early (about 9am) with a leisurely breakfast at one of the plush luxury hotels near our entrance point—the **Plaza's Palm Court** or **Edwardian Room,** the **Café Pierre at the Pierre,** or the **Fantino Restaurant at the Ritz-Carlton.** All charge about $15, including tax and tip, for a continental breakfast, $25 for a full American breakfast. Much less pricey, but still very nice, is the **Zoo Café,** just inside the park, which offers terrace seating under a wisteria arbor; it's open, as is the zoo, from 10am weekdays, from 10:30am weekends and holidays.

An advance note on meals: Although Central Park offers a few restaurants, which I'll point out as we go along, they are a bit pricey. One cheaper alternative is noshing on street food from a trail-side hot dog stand, but I enjoy bringing along the makings of a picnic.

Start at the southeastern corner of the park at **Grand Army Plaza** (see Tour 10, Stop 1). Cross 60th Street and take the wide, bench-lined path paralleling Fifth Avenue. Fork to the right, through the brick gate, and onto the path leading past the:

1. **Central Park Wildlife Conservation Center (The Central Park Zoo).** In spite of opposition by both Olmsted and Vaux, who feared losing natural scenery to gaudy attractions, there has been some sort of zoo in the park since 1864. No other American city had a zoo in the mid–19th century, and the concept was viewed as a cultural coup for New York by its founders. Originally just a diverse collection of donated animals (Olmsted mockingly opined that they were mostly "pets of children who had died"), early zoo denizens included three African Cape buffaloes acquired by General Sherman during his Georgia

Central Park

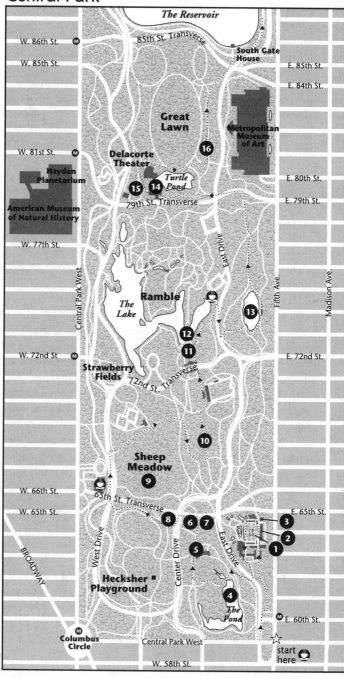

The Reservoir

W. 86th St.
W. 85th St.
85th St. Transverse
South Gate House
E. 85th St.
E. 84th St.

Great Lawn

Metropolitan Museum of Art

W. 81st St.
Hayden Planetarium
Delacorte Theater
E. 80th St.
Turtle Pond
16

American Museum of Natural History
15 **14**
79th St. Transverse
E. 79th St.

W. 77th St.

East Drive

The Lake
Ramble
13

12

Central Park West
11
E. 72nd St.

W. 72nd St
Strawberry Fields
72nd St. Transverse

Madison Ave.

Fifth Ave.

10

Sheep Meadow
9

W. 66th St.
65th St. Transverse
W. 65th St.
E. 65th St.
8 **6** **7**
3
2

West Drive
Center Drive
East Drive
5
1

BROADWAY

Hecksher Playground

4
The Pond

Columbus Circle
Central Park West
E. 60th St.
start here
W. 58th St.

7-0022

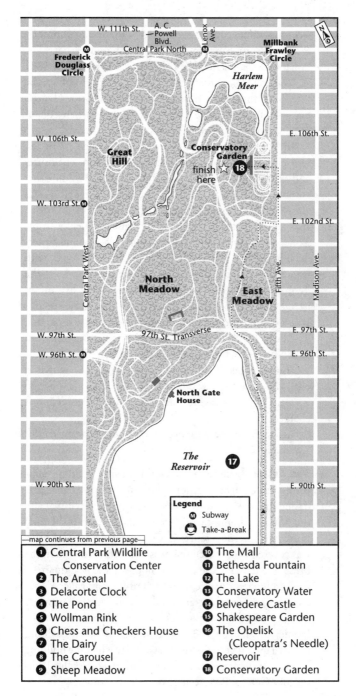

Legend
- Ⓜ Subway
- 🍵 Take-a-Break

—map continues from previous page—

1. Central Park Wildlife Conservation Center
2. The Arsenal
3. Delacorte Clock
4. The Pond
5. Wollman Rink
6. Chess and Checkers House
7. The Dairy
8. The Carousel
9. Sheep Meadow
10. The Mall
11. Bethesda Fountain
12. The Lake
13. Conservatory Water
14. Belvedere Castle
15. Shakespeare Garden
16. The Obelisk (Cleopatra's Needle)
17. Reservoir
18. Conservatory Garden

siege and circus animals quartered at the zoo in winter by P.T. Barnum. Eight monkeys (purchased rather than donated) were described in *The New York Times* in July 1871 as "comical 'Darwinian links'" (monkeys were of special interest in those early days of Darwinian theory). The zoo became a more formal establishment in 1934 when a quadrangle of redbrick animal houses was constructed.

In 1988, a renovated 5.5-acre zoo opened its doors, replacing confining cages with natural-habitat enclosures and exhibiting a cross-section of international wildlife that comprises about 450 animals. Three major ecological areas are arranged around a formal English-style Central Garden that centers on a sea lion pool. The dense, junglelike Tropic Zone, a rain-forest environment with streams and waterfalls, houses an aviary of brightly hued birds, along with monkeys, alligators, reptiles, and amphibians. In the Temperate Territory, Japanese snow monkeys live on an island in a lake inhabited by Arctic whooper swans; this area also has an outdoor pavilion for viewing red pandas. The Polar Circle is home to penguins, polar bears, harbor seals, and Arctic foxes. If you do go in, make sure to see the soothingly quiet Intelligence Garden, with wrought-iron chairs under a rustic wooden vine-covered pagoda. The zoo is open 365 days a year, 10am to 4:30pm. Admission is charged.

Across from the entrance to the zoo, up against Fifth Avenue is:

2. **The Arsenal,** a fortresslike Gothic Revival building complete with octagonal turrets. Built in the late 1840s (predating the park), it housed troops during the Civil War and was the first home of the American Museum of Natural History from 1869 to 1877. Originally, its exterior brick was covered with stucco that was later removed. Today, the brick is ivied and the Arsenal houses park headquarters, zoo administration offices, and a third-floor art gallery. Walk around to the front entrance and note the stair railing made of rifles and the weapon-related embellishments on the facade. Inside, the 1935 WPA mural by Allen Saalburg merits a look if you're here on a weekday when the building is open. It depicts maps of New York parks, idyllic 19th-century Central Park scenes, and military themes.

Walk all the way around the Arsenal to continue up the zoo pathway, arching over which is the:

3. **Delacorte Clock.** Atop an arched brick gate, this whimsical animated clock designed by Andrea Spadini has been enchanting park visitors since the mid-1960s. It features six dancing animals—a tambourine-playing bear, a kangaroo on horn, a hippo violinist, a Panlike pipe-playing goat, a penguin drummer, and an elephant squeezing an accordion. On the hour and the half hour from 8am to 6pm, the entire animal assemblage rotates to nursery rhyme tunes, and two bronze monkeys atop the clock strike a bell. "Performances" on the hour are longer.

   To get to the next stop, you'll have to double back, past the Zoo Café, and make the first right after exiting the gate, where a sign indicates the way to Wollman Rink. Bear left, cross East Drive and turn right on it, then veer left down the first sloped path you come to. Cross Gapstow Bridge over:

4. **The Pond,** originally the site of DeVoor's Mill Stream. On your left is a fenced-in bird refuge, the **Hallett Nature Sanctuary.** Where the sanctuary fence ends make a right and walk north around:

5. **Wollman Rink.** This popular skating rink, built into the northern bay of The Pond in 1951, provides skatable ice throughout the winter. The rest of the year it's drained and used for roller-skating and in-line skating. The rink's refrigerating system broke down in 1980 and remained out of operation until Donald Trump came to the rescue in 1986, bringing in his own construction specialists.

   Make the first right after the end of the rink, then the first left (an uphill slope) to the:

6. **Chess and Checkers House.** A gift from Bernard Baruch in 1952, this octagonal hilltop facility has 10 tables indoors and 24 outside for playing these games, the latter under a rustic wooden arbor covered with vines. If you neglected to bring your own chess or checker pieces, you can borrow a set, just ahead on the path and to the right, at:

7. **The Dairy.** This Gothic Revival storybook stone cottage, designed by Vaux in 1870, was originally intended to serve fresh milk and snacks to children. Cows were stabled in a

nearby building. Today, the Dairy serves as a park information center, open Tuesday to Sunday 11am to 5pm, and houses exhibits on the design and history of the park. You can pick up an events calendar and informative brochures here and check out video information terminals.

Double back, going around the right (west) side of the Chess and Checkers House. Duck through the tunnel (Playmates Arch) under Center Drive to:

8. **The Carousel.** This charming Victorian merry-go-round—originally turned by a blind mule and a horse—is one of the oldest concessions in the park. Its calliope has been playing old-fashioned tunes since 1872. The colorful whirling steeds are among the largest carousel horses in the world. Go ahead: Take the 90¢ ride.

Continuing west (take the path left of the carousel), you'll be walking past the Heckscher ball fields. When you come to West Drive, turn right (north) a short way. Tavern on the Green is across the street, behind the trees.

☕ **Take a Break** **Tavern on the Green** is located in the park at West 67th Street (☎ 212/873-3200). The original Victorian building was erected in 1870 to house the 200 sheep that grazed on the Sheep Meadow (see Stop 9). The dazzling dining room, which Mayor Fiorello LaGuardia opened with a brass key, dates from 1934. In 1976, Hollywood mogul Werner LeRoy sank $20 million in renovating the Tavern as a setting for celebrity-studded parties, film premieres, and political functions. Admittedly, when not hosting a gala event, the Tavern is basically a high-priced tourist attraction (and the food is nothing spectacular), but the sylvan setting makes for a memorable lunch atmosphere. It offers patio seating under the trees in a magnificent flower garden where 40,000 bulbs blossom year-round. There's also indoor dining, with verdant park views, in the lavish glass-enclosed Crystal Room.

Make a right on the first path you come to after Tavern on the Green as you make your way north on West Drive (a statue of 19th-century Italian revolutionary Giuseppe Mazzini is directly across the street). The path borders the:

9. **Sheep Meadow.** Originally mandated as a military parade ground, about which Olmsted was less than enthusiastic, the Sheep Meadow took on a more peaceful incarnation in 1878. Until 1934, a flock of Southdown sheep grazed here, tended by a shepherd. Though undoubtedly picturesque, the sheep became deformed from inbreeding and were banished (though only to Prospect Park in Brooklyn) by parks commissioner Robert Moses; the shepherd was reassigned to the lion house in the zoo. During the 1960s, the Sheep Meadow was a hippie haven—the setting for antiwar protests, love-ins, be-ins, and, after the 1969 Stonewall riots that launched the gay pride movement, a gay-in. Today the lush green Sheep Meadow is a popular spot for kite flyers, sunbathers, and Frisbee players—a tranquil oasis where loud radios are off limits.

Follow the fence on your right, and make a right where it turns onto the gravel path of the Lilac Walk. After you pass the volleyball court area, cross the road and look for the bronze *Indian Hunter* statue (1869) by 19th-century American artist John Quincy Adams Ward. Straight ahead (look for a group of statues), turn left up:

10. **The Mall.** Designed as a Versailles-like grand promenade, this shaded formal walkway, about a quarter of a mile in length, is bordered by a double row of stately American elms that form a cathedral arch overhead. At its entrance are statues of Columbus (created in 1892 to mark the 400th anniversary of his voyage), Shakespeare (like the *Indian Hunter,* by J.Q.A. Ward; Shakespearean actor Edwin Booth laid its cornerstone), Robert Burns, Sir Walter Scott, and American poet Fitz-Greene Halleck.

Make the first right at the end of the Mall and continue north around the back of the bandshell through the Wisteria Pergola. At the opposite end of the Mall, across East 72nd Street, a broad stairway—its massive sandstone balustrade ornately decorated with birds, flowers, and fruit—descends to one of the park's most stunning vistas:

11. **Bethesda Fountain.** Emma Stebbins's biblically inspired neoclassical winged Bethesda (the "angel of the waters") tops a vast triple-tiered stone fountain with the lake forming a scenic backdrop. Its setting is Vaux's part Gothic, part

Romanesque terrace, the heart of the park and one of its most popular venues. Like the Sheep Meadow, Bethesda Fountain was a hippie hub in the 1960s, filled with counterculture types demonstrating against the Vietnam War, smoking pot, and strumming guitars. A *Newsweek* article of that era dubbed it "Freak Fountain" and called it the "craziest, gayest, gathering place in the city." Today it is no longer a scene, but it remains one of New York's most idyllic settings.

Go down the steps (look at the balustrade's bas reliefs of the Seasons), and make a right on the path closest to:

12. **The Lake.** Its perimeter pathway lined with weeping willows and Japanese cherry trees, the 22½-acre lake was created from Sawkill Creek, which entered the Park near West 79th Street. The neo-Victorian Loeb Boathouse at the east end of the Lake rents rowboats and bicycles; evenings, you can arrange gondola rides. Along the path to the lake, you'll usually see handwriting analysts, acupressure masseurs, reflexologists, and other purveyors of New Age services.

Take a Break The **Boathouse Café** (☎ **212/ 517-2233**), at the eastern end of the Lake, is open from early spring to late October. It offers al fresco lakeside seating on a wooden deck under a white canopy. Overhead heaters allow for the cafe's extended season. The menu is contemporary American, featuring nouvelle pasta dishes, salads, focaccia sandwiches, and heartier entrees such as panfried yellowfin tuna with ginger crust. Scrumptious fresh-baked breads are a plus; however, as at Tavern on the Green, the setting is much more of a draw than the food. Lunch and brunch entrees average around $16. Lunch hours are Monday through Friday noon to 4pm and Saturday 11am to 4pm; Sunday brunch is from 11am to 4pm. An outdoor bar offers light fare, drinks, and desserts.

The cafe is very elegant, but if you want something simpler and less expensive, the Boathouse complex also houses a **cafeteria** with both indoor and outdoor seating. It serves full and continental breakfasts, sandwiches, chili, fresh fruit, and other light-fare items year-round. Hours are 9am to 6:30pm daily in summer, closing a little earlier the rest of the year.

From the south end of the Boathouse, cross East Drive and follow the path to the:

13. **Conservatory Water.** The above-mentioned Pond and Lake are free-form bodies of water. The Conservatory Water, scene of model boat races (there's even a model boathouse on the Fifth Avenue side where miniature craft are stored) is of formal design. Originally planned as the setting for a conservatory garden (built later and located further uptown; see Stop 18), it is the site of José de Creeft's *Alice in Wonderland* statues (Alice, the Mad Hatter, March Hare, Dormouse, and Cheshire Cat) inspired by the John Tenniel illustrations in the original 1865 edition. Overlooking the water is George Lober's *Hans Christian Andersen Memorial Statue,* complete with Ugly Duckling. This gift from Denmark is the setting for storytelling sessions every Saturday from June through September. Circle the pond—*Catcher in the Rye* fans will remember it as the spot where Holden Caufield came to commiserate with the ducks—and peek in the model boathouse if it's open.

Exit the Conservatory Water on the northwest path (past Alice), and continue through Glade Arch, turning left after the 79th Street Tranverse and following the path under Greywacke Arch. Ahead on the right, atop the aptly named Vista Rock, is:

14. **Belvedere Castle.** Built by Vaux in 1869, this fanciful medieval-style fortress in miniature sits at the highest point in the park and offers sweeping views across Manhattan's verdant playground. To the south, toward the lake, stretches a wild-by-design tangle of forested trails known as the **Ramble** (fun for exploring by daylight, but dangerous and seedy after dark). The many birds that call this home led to the creation of a bird-watching and educational center in the Castle's ranger station.

From Belvedere's balcony, look north over the **Delacorte Theater**, which in July and August is the setting for the popular Shakespeare in the Park series—a pair of plays each summer performed by both headliner stars (Denzel Washington, Christopher Walken) and eminent Shakespearean thespians (Patrick Stewart did a *Tempest* turn in 1995). Although shows start at 8pm, tickets are free, so it's wise to show up before noon and wait until the box office opens at

1pm to snag a pair. Beyond the Delacorte, and undergoing restoration in 1997, stretches the **Great Lawn,** host to some of New York's most famous blowout events, including Paul Simon's gratis Concert in the Park.

Just past the castle, and before the Swedish Cottage Marionette Theater (puppet shows July to mid August, Monday to Friday at 10:30am and noon), nestles the:

15. **Shakespeare Garden,** where the only flowers and plants in evidence are those mentioned in the Bard's plays.

Double back along the 79th St. Transverse to turn left (north) up the East Drive (just before Greywacke Arch). Up ahead, across from the backside of the Metropolitan Museums, rises:

16. **The Obelisk (Cleopatra's Needle).** This 3,500-year-old, 77-foot-high, Egyptian pink granite obelisk was a gift to New York City from the khedive of Egypt in 1881 to thank America for its help in building the Suez Canal. William Vanderbilt paid the cost of transportation (over $100,000), a complicated affair that involved the construction of a railroad track from the Hudson River. The obelisk immediately became a major park attraction; gazing upon it, noted the *Herald,* "was regarded as a far greater treat by the majority of park visitors than to watch the wondrous developments of nature."

Dating from the reign of King Thutmose III in 1600 B.C., the obelisk stood in front of the Temple of the Sun in Heliopolis, Egypt, until it was removed by the Romans in 12 B.C. and placed at the approach of a temple built by Cleopatra (hence its nickname). Its hieroglyphics (which are translated here, a gift of Cecil B. de Mille) tell of the deeds of Thutmose III, Ramses II, and Osarkon I. The four bronze crabs peeking out from each corner of the base are 19th-century replicas of the originals, which it is believed were placed there by the Romans as a decorative means of support. Crabs were objects of worship to the ancient Egyptians.

Follow the path behind (west of) the obelisk. When it ends, bear right and follow East Drive, keeping to the left. Soon you'll come to steps and a cast-iron bridge leading to the South Gate House. Make a right onto the jogging path of the:

17. **Reservoir,** created in 1862 to supply New York City's water system. Occupying 106 acres and extending the width of the park, it is girded by bridle and jogging paths. The reservoir holds a billion gallons of water, is 40 feet at its greatest depth, and now serves only as an emergency back-up water supply. The path around it is 1.57 miles long. Walk or jog along the eastern border of the reservoir, getting off at 96th Street (a playground is diagonally across).

Continue north on East Drive to 102nd Street, exit the park, and walk north along Fifth Avenue to the Vanderbilt Gate. This ornate portal, designed in Paris in 1894, formerly heralded the Fifth Avenue mansion of Cornelius Vanderbilt II. Fittingly adorned with plant motifs, it is the entrance to the:

18. **Conservatory Garden.** This formal garden was originally the site of a complex of glass greenhouses built in 1899. Its symmetrical paths and arbor walks contrast with the natural look of the rest of the park. They were dismantled in 1934, when parks commissioner Robert Moses deemed maintenance costs too high. He commissioned the current garden as a WPA project in 1936. As you enter from Fifth Avenue, you'll be facing the elegant Italian garden—a greensward centered on a classical fountain. It is ringed with yew hedges and bordered by allées of Siberian crabapple trees. In spring the crabapples bloom with pink and white flowers and narcissus grows in the ivy beneath them.

Walk through the allée on the left to the lovely mazelike English garden. It contains the bronze statue of the children from *The Secret Garden* standing in a reflecting pool. In summer there are water lilies and a wide variety of flowering plants and shrubs. Now walk through the Wisteria Pergola (at the back of the Italian garden). This flower-bedecked wrought-iron arbor, especially magnificent in late May, connects the English and French gardens.

In the French garden, entered via rose-covered arched trellises, two levels of flower beds encircle the Untermeyer Fountain that centers on an enchanting sculpture of dancing maidens by Walter Schott. Here 20,000 tulips bloom in spring and 5,000 chrysanthemums in fall.

The Upper West Side

Start: 86th Street and Broadway.

Subway: Take the 1 or 9 to 86th Street.

Finish: Lincoln Center.

Time: 3½ hours (allow more time for shopping, refreshment stops, and museum visits).

Best Time: Weekday afternoons, when shops and museums are open but crowds are at a minimum.

The Upper West Side has undergone a decidedly upwardly mobile transformation in the last few decades. Though some magnificent luxury apartment buildings have stood here since the days of gaslights and horse-drawn carriages, for the first half of the 20th century, they were surrounded by an otherwise unremarkable, largely working-class neighborhood. Then came Lincoln Center.

A massive urban renewal effort centered around the construction of this performing arts complex in the early 1960s. Blocks of dilapidated housing and bodegas gave way to pricey boutiques and exclusive residential buildings.

Gentrification almost completely swallowed up the West Side in the decades that followed, but dozens of mom-and-pop dry cleaners and shoe repair shops still remain, giving the West Side its unique flavor. Especially as you go further uptown, you might spot a neighborhood barber shop still going strong even though a trendy new hair salon has opened nearby, or you'll suddenly come upon a block where the signs are in Spanish and the sounds of salsa blast from everyone's windows.

Some old-timers bemoan the changes, but after the yuppie invasion of the 1970s and 1980s, the West Side has maintained a more democratic and informal atmosphere than the stuffy East Side. This is the neighborhood inhabited by the characters on *Seinfeld,* and it pulses with life. Residents pride themselves on the wonderful food shopping at Fairway and Zabar's; they can enjoy an authentic Cuban dinner in a simple hole in the wall one night and dine in an elegant French bistro or a sleek sushi bar the next.

• • • • • • • • • • • • • • • •

From the 86th Street subway station, walk south down the east side of Broadway to 84th Street ("Edgar Allan Poe Street"). Just off Broadway to your left is:

1. **215 West 84th St.** As recently as the 1840s, this area was still undeveloped rural countryside. Edgar Allan Poe lived briefly with his wife in a farmhouse that stood here on a rocky knoll. He completed *The Raven* here in the summer of 1844.

Go back to Broadway and cross the street; turn left, heading downtown. At the northwest corner of 80th Street and Broadway stands:

2. **Zabar's** (☎ 212/787-2000) a West Side retail institution. The faint of heart should beware: Zabar's is sheer bedlam, and its crowd of serious shoppers will shove you right out of the way for the perfect wheel of Brie. But plunge into the crowds and wander through the aisles for a mind-boggling selection of imported cheeses, breads, cold cuts, salads, and appetizers. The aroma of freshly ground coffee pervades the store. At the fish counter, you can get anything from smoked salmon to caviar. If you're taking this

The Upper West Side

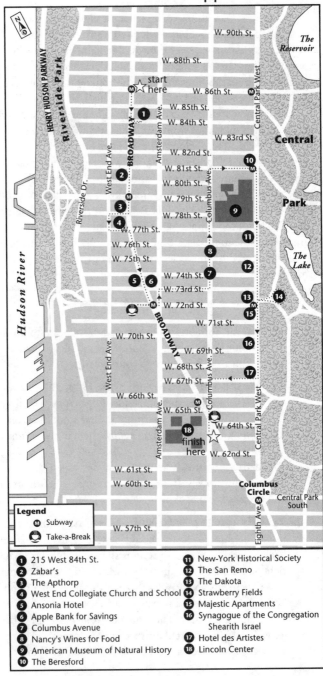

Legend
- Ⓜ Subway
- 🥣 Take-a-Break

1. 215 West 84th St.
2. Zabar's
3. The Apthorp
4. West End Collegiate Church and School
5. Ansonia Hotel
6. Apple Bank for Savings
7. Columbus Avenue
8. Nancy's Wines for Food
9. American Museum of Natural History
10. The Beresford
11. New-York Historical Society
12. The San Remo
13. The Dakota
14. Strawberry Fields
15. Majestic Apartments
16. Synagogue of the Congregation Shearith Israel
17. Hotel des Artistes
18. Lincoln Center

tour on a beautiful spring day, you'll find the fixings here for a memorable picnic feast in Central Park (coming up later on the tour).

Don't be daunted either by the long lines you are sure to see emanating from **H&H Bagels,** just across 80th Street. As anyone in the neighborhood will tell you, these are a favorite front-runner for the coveted title of best bagels in New York—so fresh they're still warm from the oven.

Just south rises the magnificent, 1908 limestone faca de of:

3. **The Apthorp,** which commands an entire square block bounded by 78th and 79th streets, Broadway, and West End Avenue. Admire the 1908 building from the Broadway side, standing in front of the stately iron gates that lead into a landscaped central courtyard with a pair of fountains, marble benches, and statuary. You may recognize it from a conga line of New York–based films in which the Apthorp featured, including *Rosemary's Baby, The Cotton Club, Heartburn, The Money Pit,* and *Network.*

Turn right and take 78th Street west, heading away from the bustle of Broadway. Then turn left down West End Avenue. At the northeast corner of 77th Street stands the Flemish-style:

4. **West End Collegiate Church and School,** with dormer windows and a steep red-tiled roof. The church was completed in 1892 for the Collegiate Reformed Protestant Dutch Church, a congregation formed by Dutch colonists in 1628. The Collegiate School, established by the church in 1638, is one of the oldest independent secondary schools in the country, and still functions as one of New York's posher prep schools.

Proceed east on 77th Street back to Broadway and head downtown. At the corner of 75th Street sits **Citarella** (☎ 212/874-0383), another excellent gourmet food shop that in 1997 opened a second floor and began really giving Zabar's a run for the money. At 74th Street, you'll pass **Fairway,** West Siders' favorite produce store. Even in winter, fresh fruits and vegetables abound here, and it's usually a hectic bustle inside. A block further south, you'll see the splendid beaux arts–style:

5. **Ansonia Hotel,** between 73rd and 74th streets, built as a luxury residential hotel and completed in 1904. Its architect, W.E.D. Stokes, bought this parcel of land, then surrounded by single-family homes, and decided to raise eyebrows by building a 17-story "tenement" in flamboyant French style. Resembling a lacy, opulent wedding cake, the Ansonia sports a three-story mansard roof and rounded corner towers capped with high domes.

Luxurious apartment houses were all the rage at the turn of the century, and the Ansonia's early tenants were lured by an incredible series of amenities and services. Messages propelled pneumatically in a network of tubes could be sent from room to room. There was a grand ballroom, a swimming pool, a trellised roof garden, a theater, a barber shop, a pharmacist, a florist, and a laundry. Live seals splashed about in the lobby's fountain. There were several restaurants where tenants could dine or have meals sent up to their suites. Stokes himself kept a small pet bear, goats, and chickens in the roof garden; he sold the eggs to tenants at a discount.

The Ansonia has always been a favorite address for musicians, among them Stravinsky, Toscanini, and Caruso. (The apartments here are virtually soundproof, so musicians can practice without fear of disturbing other tenants.)

The golden age of the Ansonia ended with the Great Depression, and the building has slid into decline marked by legal battles between tenants and owners. It was, however, declared a landmark in 1972. (You may recognize it as the setting for the thriller *Single White Female.*)

Just downtown from the Ansonia on 72nd Street is **HMV,** a music superstore with three floors of CDs, tapes, and videos—everything from Louis Armstrong to ZZ Top.

Take a Break Tucked away in a basement on the downtown side of 72nd Street between Broadway and West End Avenue is a pub that hosts a crowd of neighborhood regulars. The **All State Cafe,** 250 West 72nd St. (☎ 212/874-1883), serves typical bar food—fried calamari, spicy chicken wings, and bowls of chili—plus surprisingly good daily specials. The thick, juicy burgers are among the best in town. Peter the bartender makes a mean margarita, and offers an impressive selection of whiskies. If you're there on a chilly winter day, you'll appreciate the fire crackling in the hearth beside the bar. And there's a great selection of classic rock, jazz, oldies, and swing tunes on the jukebox. The All State is open daily from 11:30am to 1am (later on weekends).

While you're munching on your burger, ponder this: in the early 1970s, this joint was H.M. Tweed's singles bar. On New Year's Day 1973, schoolteacher Roseanne Quinn picked up a guy named John Wayne Wilson and figured he'd make a good one-night stand. After he strangled and stabbed her, he was arrested, confessed, and committed suicide while awaiting trial. The book and movie inspired by the murder, *Looking for Mr. Goodbar,* became an anthem against the casual sex culture of the '70s.

Go back to Broadway and 73rd Street; now take 73rd Street east and cross Broadway. Between 73rd and 74th streets is the:

6. **Apple Bank for Savings,** designed by York and Sawyer in the 1920s and boasting a massive limestone facade and stunning ironwork doors. The structure's trapezoid shape allows it to fill out the plot of land created where Broadway cuts diagonally across Amsterdam Avenue. And its heavy, monumental style is perfectly suited to a bank building. You'll pass beneath a decorative clock, topped with twin lions.

Continue east on 73rd Street to:

7. **Columbus Avenue,** one of New York's trendiest promenades, lined with boutiques, coffee bars, and restaurants. Stores spring up like weeds on Columbus—and they disa-ppear as fast as yesterday's news. Take this part of the stroll to stop and browse in any place that catches your eye. Exotiqa II (no. 284) offers international crafts (look for the colorful Indonesian cats). Try Profiles (no. 294) and Kenneth Cole (no. 353) for up-to-the-minute styles in shoes. There's Variazioni (no. 309) and Putumayo (no. 341) for women's fashions, but my favorite shop on this stretch is:

8. **Nancy's Wines for Food,** at no. 313 (☎ 212/877-4040). Nancy's is one of the few wine shops that doesn't pull the restaurant stunt of making a 400% or higher profit from

each bottle. There are usually more than 100 labels of wine in stock under $10, and those that are pricier are generally worth it. Each wine is marked with an index card describing its qualities and usually what foods it best accompanies. There's no enological snobbery here; just good, plainspoken advice, excellent wines, and unbelievable prices. Nancy's is open Monday to Thursday 10am to 9pm, Friday and Saturday 10am to 10pm.

While you're meandering up Columbus, take a peek off to your left at **150 West 75th St.,** where Anaîs Nin lived with her mother and brother from 1914 to 1919. In the first-floor rooming house at this address, the teenage writer began penning the diary that became her most important work.

Continue your stroll up Columbus, taking your time to allow for optimum people-watching. At 77th Street, take a right. This block was described in Tom Wolfe's *Bonfire of the Vanities* as the most beautiful in town. Halfway down it is the entrance to the:

9. **American Museum of Natural History** (☎ 212/ 769-5100), home to 36 million artifacts of Earth's history. The famous Hall of Dinosaurs, housing several skeletons of our prehistoric predecessors, is a perennial hit still basking in the renaissance of dino-interest brought by the *Jurassic Park* film empire (didactic to the last, the museum labors at many of the high-tech saurian exhibits to correct gently the film's paleontological errors and other general dinosaur misconceptions). Other highlights include, at the heart of an astounding minerals and gems section, the largest meteorite ever retrieved, and an impressive collection of pre-Columbian artifacts. This last brings up a sticky but interesting point: the museum is saddled by tradition to function, in part, as what should better be termed an ethnology museum. The very fact that they have whole sections devoted to Haida dugout canoes and totem poles highlights the ludicrously racist notion that, while European and Mediterranean art and cultural output can be displayed at the Metropolitan and other fine art museums across the park, the cultural histories of the "primitive" peoples of the Americas, Africa, and Asia are somehow considered "natural history." However, throughout the museum,

plaques, films, and CD-ROM terminals go to great pains to point out the museum's own history of embarrassing errors, and to teach how what we consider "scientific fact" is really just opinion grounded in the thinking of a particular era. The suggested admission is worth it; the museum's hours are Sunday to Thursday 10am to 5:45pm, Friday and Saturday 10am to 8:45pm.

Head back to Columbus Avenue and continue north to 81st Street. Make a right and head toward Central Park West, passing no. 11, whose apartments are home to actresses Teri Garr and Natassia Kinski. Further ahead on your left, crowning the northwest corner of the intersection, is:

10. **The Beresford,** the first in a long line of architectural gems you'll pass on Central Park West. The Beresford, with its baroque tower and classical ornamentation, is an adaptation of an Italian Renaissance palazzo. Its architect, Emery Roth, was a Jewish immigrant who arrived in this country flat broke as a teenager. He taught himself design and, through sheer hard work and determination, became one of the city's most noted architects.

Apartments at the Beresford are hard to come by and run into the millions of dollars. Gangster Meyer Lansky lived here in the 1940s, and more recently, actor Rock Hudson lived here until his death from AIDS in 1985. Other famous residents have included Margaret Mead, who used to walk to work nearby at the Museum of Natural History, plus Tony Randall, ABC anchor Peter Jennings, his colleague Diane Sawyer, and Helen Gurley Brown.

Turn right and head down Central Park West. (Turn back and look up at the Beresford after a half block or so for a better perspective.) Along here is another entrance to the Museum of Natural History, marked by an equestrian statue of Teddy Roosevelt. At the southwest corner of 77th Street and Central Park West, you'll see the:

11. **New-York Historical Society** (☎ 212/873-3400), a rich repository of artifacts, artworks, and documents that chronicle the city's history. Established in 1804, it is New York's oldest museum. In addition to its renowned research library, the museum's highlights include John James Audubon's original *Birds of America* watercolor series, a

gallery of more than 150 Tiffany lamps, and an extensive collection of early American art. They charge admission, and hours are Wednesday to Sunday noon to 5pm.

From here, cross Central Park West to walk down the park side to better view the buildings we're about to pass. Between 74th and 75th streets stands:

12. **The San Remo,** 145–146 Central Park West, once home to heavyweight boxing champ Jack Dempsey and pinup idol Rita Hayworth, the San Remo is another grand apartment building bearing the stamp of Emery Roth. The two towers rising at each end are crowned with columned temples. After struggling through the Depression, the owners sold the San Remo and the Beresford together in 1940 for the shocking sum of $25,000 over the combined mortgages. More recent residents include an A-list of actors—Dustin Hoffman, Mary Tyler Moore, Bruce Willis and Demi Moore, Diane Keaton, and Steve Martin—along with popular crooner Barry Manilow.

At Central Park West and 72nd Street is a world-famous architectural masterpiece:

13. **The Dakota,** one of the first luxury apartment buildings in New York, built in 1880–84. Legend has it that the building's name came about when Edward S. Clark, the project's developer, was teased by his friends that the site was so far north of the city center that it might as well have been in Dakota territory. Architect Henry J. Hardenbergh, who also designed New York's landmark Plaza Hotel, created a brooding, Germanic structure accented with gables, dormers, and oriel windows, surrounded by a "dry moat." The fortresslike building is so atmospheric that it served as the backdrop to the horror movie *Rosemary's Baby.*

The list of tenants at this prestigious address has included Lauren Bacall, Leonard Bernstein, Connie Chung, John Madden, and Roberta Flack, and Boris Karloff (whose ghost reputedly haunts the halls). But the Dakota will forever be associated with its most famous resident, John Lennon, who was gunned down just outside the building.

Lennon was returning home to the Dakota after a recording session on December 8, 1980, when he was shot by Mark David Chapman, a lone psychopath who had asked for the former Beatle's autograph only hours earlier. Lennon's widow, Yoko Ono, still lives in the Dakota.

Just inside the 72nd Street entrance to Central Park lies:

14. **Strawberry Fields,** a memorial to Lennon built and maintained by his widow. The three-acre teardrop-shaped "international garden of peace" is adorned with more than 150 species of plants (gifts from as many nations) and 2,500 strawberry plants. Near the entrance, a circular black-and-white tile mosaic—a gift from Naples, Italy—spells out the word "Imagine."

As you exit the park to continue on your route downtown, you'll be right across the street from the:

15. **Majestic Apartments,** 115 Central Park West, another of the grand apartment houses that define the Central Park West skyline. Until the 12-story Hotel Majestic was built in the 1890s, this site was occupied by wooden shacks and grazing goats. It became however, a sumptuous venue that hosted the likes of Sarah Bernhardt, Edna Ferber, Gustav Mahler, and Vaslav Nijinsky. In 1929, developer Irwin Chanin initiated plans to build a single-tower, 45-story structure. The months that followed, however, saw the stock market crash, so Chanin altered his plans and came up with the 29-story, twin-towered structure you see today between 71st and 72nd streets. He also broke with tradition by scorning the classical European models used for most large residential buildings in New York; instead he chose an adaptation of art deco style he called Modern American. The building was ready for tenants in 1931, but the Depression grew so severe that Chanin had defaulted on his mortgage by 1933.

Although it's had its share of famous residents, including Fred Astaire, Isadora Duncan, and Milton Berle, the Majestic is also connected to two major scandals. Bruno Richard Hauptmann, prosecuted for kidnapping the Lindbergh baby, was working as a carpenter here when the crime was committed. And a gangland hit took place in the lobby in 1957, when mobster Frank Costello was shot in the head (fellow gangsters Lucky Luciano and Meyer Lansky also called the Majestic home for a while).

Further down Central Park West, at the southwest corner of 70th Street, you'll see the:

16. **Synagogue of the Congregation Shearith Israel,**
    which dates from 1897. It's home to the oldest Jewish con-
    gregation in the United States, founded in 1654 by Span-
    ish and Portuguese immigrants who came to New York via
    Brazil.

    Turn right onto 67th Street, where several buildings
    contain double-height studio apartments. At no. 1 is the
    Gothic-style:

17. **Hotel des Artistes,** full of enchanting touches, such as
    the row of gargoyles found below the third-floor windows.

    Most of the units in the Hotel des Artistes are duplexes
    and double-height studios. One particularly noteworthy
    apartment, designed for philanthropist Aaron Naumburg
    and completed in 1921, has 18-foot ceilings, a wood-
    balustraded balcony, and lavishly carved woodwork.
    Naumberg's home was graced with tapestries, fine carpets,
    antique Italian furniture, paintings, carved figures, and
    stained-glass windows—and so spectacular was it that all
    the furnishings and artwork were taken to the Fogg Mu-
    seum in Cambridge and re-created as an annex after
    Naumberg's death.

    The Hotel des Artistes has attracted an astounding num-
    ber of famous residents, including Rudolph Valentino, Nôel
    Coward, Isadora Duncan, Alexander Woolcott, Edna Ferber,
    former mayor John Lindsay, former governor Hugh Carey,
    Norman Rockwell, and Emil Fuchs, portraitist to Queen
    Victoria. Fuchs, dying of cancer, committed suicide in the
    Hotel des Artistes in 1929 by shooting himself with a pearl-
    handled revolver inscribed by Edward VII. More grisliness
    ensued on December 10, 1929, when bohemian poet Harry
    Crosby killed both his girlfriend and himself in a ninth-
    floor apartment.

    The ground floor houses the elegant and romantic **Café
    des Artistes;** peek in the window to see the restaurant's
    famous wood-nymph murals by Howard Chandler Christy,
    a longtime tenant in the building. (Some of the models
    used for the nymphs have returned to dine in the cafe over
    the years.) Christy's murals and his other depictions of lovely
    ladies in magazine and book illustrations earned him an
    invitation to be the sole judge at the first Miss America
    contest.

Continue west on 67th Street to Columbus Avenue and make a left. Between 65th and 66th streets stands the **Museum of American Folk Art** annex and its gift shop (☎ **212/496-2966**), stocked with books, jewelry, hand-painted pitchers and vases, prints, and one-of-a-kind greeting cards. Across Broadway, you can't miss:

18. **Lincoln Center,** the city's premier venue for the performing arts. In 1956, a committee headed by John D. Rockfeller III selected the site for Lincoln Center, in what was then a rundown residential area. *West Side Story* was filmed in these streets before an astounding 188 buildings were demolished to clear the area; 1,600 people had to be relocated to make way for the project.

The committee commissioned a group of architects headed by Wallace K. Harrison; each building they created has classical lines, and is covered in Italian travertine (unfortunately, although the exteriors may be elegant, music lovers, critics, and performers complain of the banal acoustics in the actual performance halls). The centerpiece of the complex is an outdoor plaza graced with a cafe terrace and a splashing fountain. New Yorkers enjoy free entertainment under the stars here on the plaza in summer, and in December, one of the city's most beautiful Christmas trees is mounted here.

Left of the plaza is Avery Fisher Hall, with a peristyle of 44 columns soaring seven stories high. It's home to the New York Philharmonic, which has counted among its musical directors such luminaries as Zubin Mehta, Arturo Toscanini, Leopold Stokowski, and Leonard Bernstein. On the right side of the fountain is the New York State Theater, designed by architect Philip Johnson, which hosts performances by the New York City Opera and the New York City Ballet, which was founded by George Balanchine.

Forming the background of the plaza is the Metropolitan Opera House, which boasts a marble colonnade 10 stories high. Inside the glass facade, you can see two enormous murals by Marc Chagall. This is the home of the renowned Metropolitan Opera, one of the most prestigious companies in the world for more than a century; acclaimed stars such as Placido Domingo, Luciano Pavarotti, Jose Carreras, Kathleen Battle, and Marilyn Horne have graced the stage here. In early summer, the Opera House also hosts the American Ballet Theatre's season. The Met's interior houses seven rehearsal halls and space to store scenery for as many as 15 operas.

The remainder of the complex at Lincoln Center includes the Guggenheim Bandshell, used for free outdoor concerts; the Vivian Beaumont and Mitzi Newhouse Theaters; the Julliard School, the country's premier academy for the performing arts; and Alice Tully Hall. Also at Lincoln Center is a branch of the New York Public Library, which serves as both a library and a museum of the performing arts. The library hosts an impressive array of free films and concerts.

One-hour tours of Lincoln Center are offered for a small fee; call ☎ **212/875-5350** to check on the day's tour schedule and to make advance reservations. Calendars of upcoming events, including free concerts, are available.

Winding Down Almost any craving can be satisfied at **The Saloon,** 1920 Broadway, at 64th Street (☎ **212/874-1500**), where the specialty is light, creative American and continental fare—and the prices are jacked up to take advantage of the after-theater crowd. The kitchen is rather uneven—the menu is so large that the more ambitious offerings sometimes fail—but the basic salads, burgers, individual pizzas, and sandwiches are all dependably good. In summer the outdoor cafe tables offer great people-watching. You'll occasionally see the roller-skating waiters and waitresses dodging tables, diners, and the many passersby who crowd this street.

The Upper East Side

Start: The southeast corner of Central Park, at 59th Street and Fifth Avenue.

Subway: Take the N or R to Fifth Avenue.

Finish: 91st Street and Fifth Avenue.

Time: Approximately 3 hours.

Best Time: Weekday afternoons, when museums and restaurants are open but not as crowded as on Saturdays.

Worst Time: Sundays, when most stores and galleries are closed and the streets seem deserted.

Over a century ago, society watchers predicted that the wealthy and fashionable would settle permanently on the avenues bordering Central Park. Time has proven them right. Fifth Avenue north of Grand Army Plaza, which lies at the southeast corner of the park, is officially called Museum Mile. But the magnificent private mansions built here in the first few decades of this century by some of America's wealthiest industrial tycoons also earned it the title of Millionaires' Row. Judging from old photos, it was something to behold.

Today, patrician mansions still stand along the avenue, though others have ceded their coveted real estate to large apartment houses. But the age of imperial living isn't over by any means. Some of the buildings on Fifth (as well as on Park Avenue and elsewhere on the East Side) contain apartments every bit as palatial and sumptuous as the vanished mansions. Even New Yorkers are surprised to hear of apartments with 20, 30, or even 40 rooms—but they do exist in this neighborhood.

• • • • • • • • • • • • • • • •

Start your tour where Fifth Avenue and 59th Street meet:

1. **Grand Army Plaza,** adorned with a brilliant gold statue of William Tecumseh Sherman, the ruthless but effective Civil War general who devastated the Southern countryside and brought the civilian population to its knees with the Union army's scorched-earth "March to the Sea." "War is cruelty and you cannot refine it," Sherman once observed, but sculptor Augustus Saint-Gaudens has tried. He's created a classical equestrian statue of the crusty general with a female Winged Victory striding along in front of the horse. It was unveiled on Memorial Day 1903, with bands playing *Marching Through Georgia* and a military parade (some of Sherman's men were among the marchers). This is the patriotic (victorious Union) view of the statue. But truth is in the eye of the beholder, and a popular story goes that a proper Southern lady, upon being told whom the statue represented, harumphed, "Ain't that just like a Yankee, to make the lady walk."

    Now stroll up Fifth Avenue, staying on the park side of the street for the best view of the buildings we'll be passing. In good weather bookstalls from The Strand line the sidewalk, full of used volumes at a fraction of the cover price. On the east (right) side of Fifth Avenue, at 61st Street, is:

2. **The Pierre,** one of Manhattan's priciest and most exclusive hotels since its opening in 1930. In 1932, mystery writer Dashiell Hammett stayed here while working on *The Thin Man,* though, unfortunately, he couldn't pay the bill that he had run up during his stay. He allegedly donned a disguise to sneak out without settling his tab.

The Upper East Side

Legend
- Ⓜ Subway
- ☕ Take-a-Break

The Reservoir

E. 92nd St.
E. 90th St.
E. 88th St.
E. 86th St.
E. 84th St.
E. 82nd St.
E. 79th St.
E. 78th St.
E. 77th St.
E. 76th St.
E. 75th St.
E. 74th St.
E. 73rd St.
E. 72nd St.
E. 71st St.
E. 70th St.
E. 69th St.
E. 68th St.
E. 67th St.
E. 66th St.
E. 65th St.
E. 64th St.
E. 63rd St.
E. 62nd St.
E. 61st St.
E. 60th St.
E. 59th St.

☆ finish here

☆ start here

YORKVILLE

Gracie Mansion

Carl Schurz Park

Metropolitan Museum of Art

Central Park

Fifth Ave.
Madison Ave.
Park Ave.
Lexington Ave.
Third Ave.
Second Ave.
First Ave.
York Ave.

FDR Drive

East River

Grand Army Plaza

Queensboro Bridge

7-0024

1. Grand Army Plaza
2. The Pierre
3. Knickerbocker Club
4. 820 Fifth Ave.
5. The Arsenal
6. 3 East 64th St.
7. Home of Ulysses S. Grant
8. 58 East 68th St.
9. 680 Park Ave.
10. Union Club
11. East 70th Street
12. Asia Society
13. Frick Collection
14. Polo/Ralph Lauren
15. 11 East 73rd St.
16. Whitney Museum of American Art
17. 972 Fifth Ave.
18. Metropolitan Museum of Art
19. Home of Jacqueline Kennedy Onassis
20. 86th Street
21. Guggenheim Museum
22. Cooper-Hewitt National Design Museum
23. Convent of the Sacred Heart

155

If you're starting out early in the morning, breakfast at the Pierre makes for a pricey but elegant beginning to your tour.

At the southeast corner of 62nd Street stands the third home of the:

3. **Knickerbocker Club,** which looks a lot like the big private houses that once characterized the avenue. The Georgian brick Knickerbocker, completed in 1915, was the work of a firm called Delano and Aldrich, a favorite of high society in the early 20th century. It retains a very pedigreed image. Ernest Hemingway, looking for peace and quiet, rented an apartment here in 1959, and stayed for about a year.

The next block up is 63rd Street and just north of it you'll see:

4. **820 Fifth Ave.,** one of the earliest apartment houses built hereabouts and still one of the best. Built in 1916, it has only one apartment on each floor, with five fireplaces and seven bathrooms in each.

Continue northward on Fifth Avenue to 64th Street. Walk just inside Central Park for a look at:

5. **The Arsenal,** built in 1848 when this neighborhood was distant and deserted. Now housing zoo administration offices, the structure was once a bunkhouse for Civil War troops (see Tour 8, Stop 2). The **Central Park Zoo** is right behind the building.

Head back onto Fifth Avenue. Opposite the park, at the southeast corner of 64th Street, is the former mansion of coal magnate Edward Berwind. If you've seen the mansions in Newport, Rhode Island, you've probably already seen Mr. Berwind's summer house, the Elms. His New York residence dates from 1896 and has been preserved as cooperative apartments.

Head east (away from the park) on 64th Street toward Madison Avenue. This is a particularly handsome East Side block, lined with architectural extravaganzas. Note in particular:

6. **3 East 64th St.,** an opulent beaux arts mansion built in 1903 for the daughter of Mrs. William B. Astor. The house was designed by Warren and Wetmore, the firm responsible for Grand Central Terminal, and it now houses the

Consulate General of India. Also worthy of admiration on this block are nos. 16, 19, and 20.

At Madison Avenue, turn left and saunter two blocks north to 66th Street. Note the rather fantastic apartment house built in 1900 on the northeast corner of 66th and Madison, then turn left (west) off Madison onto 66th Street, heading back toward Fifth Avenue.

Among the many notable houses on this block is the magnificent French Renaissance–style house at 5 East 66th St., with its heavy wooden doors and elegant stonework detail. Built in 1900, it's now home to the Lotos Club, dedicated to literature and the fine arts.

Next door, at 3 East 66th St., is the:

7. **Home of President Ulysses S. Grant,** where he lived from 1881 to 1885. Forced to declare bankruptcy after a disastrous presidency that was marred by scandal, the former Civil War hero retired here to spend his last years penning his personal memoirs. Though he was battling cancer, Grant managed to hang on just long enough to complete the autobiography, which won favorable literary reviews and earned his family half a million dollars.

Now double back to Madison Avenue, turn left, and continue north for two more blocks, stopping to browse in any of the boutiques that catch your eye. There's Nicole Miller; La Perla for lovely lingerie; Emanuel Ungaro; Godiva, which offers a few cafe tables for lingering over coffee and a decadent truffle; Monaco for cashmere; and Peter Fox for the priciest boots this side of Dallas. At 68th Street, turn right (east) toward Park Avenue. One of the best houses on this block is:

8. **58 East 68th St.,** on the southwest corner of the intersection with Park Avenue. The house was built in 1919 for Harold J. Pratt, son of Rockefeller partner Charles Pratt.

Walk to the north side of 68th Street to:

9. **680 Park Ave.,** a neo-Federal town house, built in 1909–11 for banker Percy Rivington Pyne and designed by McKim, Mead, and White. Its style and architecture was copied all along this Park Avenue block front. When, from 1948 to 1963, it housed the Soviet Mission to the United Nations, Premier Nikita Krushchev waved to curious crowds

from the balcony during his famous shoe-banging visit to the U.N.

The Marquesa de Cuevas bought 680 Park Ave. in 1965, staving off a slated demolition by presenting it to the Americas Society. The society is the only national not-for-profit institution devoted to educating U.S. citizens about their western hemisphere neighbors. The society sponsors public art exhibitions and cultural programs on Latin American and Canadian affairs.

Head north on Park Avenue to 69th Street, where, on the northeast corner, is the:

10. **Union Club,** designed in 1932 to house New York's oldest club. On the other side of 69th Street is Hunter College. Turn right onto 69th Street and continue east toward Lexington Avenue, noting en route 117 East 69th St., a prototypical not-so-small private East Side house with beautiful stained-glass panels around the door.

When you arrive at Lexington Avenue, detour right half a block to a still-operating branch of **Shakespeare and Co.** (no. 939), Manhattan's famously literary bookseller whose West Side main branch was put out of business in 1996 when Barnes and Noble strategically built two megastores within walking distance. Double back up Lexington 1½ blocks uptown to 70th Street. Turn left and head back toward Park Avenue along:

11. **East 70th Street,** which presents a succession of elegant houses, each more beautiful than the next. Some consider this the finest street in New York. Note in particular no. 125, a post–World War II mansion built for Paul Mellon in a French provincial style.

When you arrive at the Park Avenue end of the block, note the modern building on the northeast corner housing the:

12. **Asia Society,** which offers workshops, lectures, films, and performances on Asian culture. Major art exhibitions, both ancient and contemporary, are held in the galleries; admission is charged.

Cross Park and note **720 Park Ave.,** on the northwest corner of the intersection. This is a prime example of the sort of swanky, enormous apartment building that lured former mansion dwellers away from their private houses. The upper floors of buildings like no. 720 often contain apartments with three or four floors and dozens of rooms.

Continue on East 70th Street toward Fifth Avenue. Two of the upper east side's premier art galleries are along here. **Hirschl and Adler** at no. 21 shows quality works of American and European art in many media ranging from the 18th century to current day masterpieces. The ground floor houses the big old guns, from John Singleton Copley, Winsolow Homer, Edward Hopper, and Georgia O'Keeffe to Mary Cassatt, Picasso, and Renoir. The second floor, modern art branch shows the works of Southern black folk artist Forrest Bess, performing artist team Gilbert and George, and other artists like John Moore and Fairfield Porter. Next door, at no. 19, is **Knoedler and Company**, a major gallery for established American artists like Helen Frankenthaler, Adolph Gottlieb, Nancy Graves, Frank Stella, and John Walker.

Nearing Fifth Avenue, you'll pass a lovely courtyard and lily pond, surrounded by stately black iron gates, before reaching the entrance to my favorite New York museum, the:

13. **Frick Collection** (☎ 212/288-0700), housed in the 1914 mansion of steel magnate Henry Clay Frick and very evocative of the gilded age. The beautiful classic garden overlooking 70th Street was built in 1977. Frick always intended that his art collection be opened to the public after his death. The works are arrayed in rooms, many with Frick's original furnishings, centered around a small, plant-filled atrium with classical styling, a vaulted skylight, and a softly splashing fountain. If you only have time for one museum on this tour, the modestly sized but rich Frick may be your best choice.

The collections range from Italian medieval (a panel from Duccio's *Maestà*) and the Renaissance (Piero della Francesca, Bellini, Bronzino, Titian, and El Greco), to later French, Spanish, Flemish, German, and American masterpieces from the likes of Rembrandt, Ingres, Gainsborough, Boucher, Goya, Whistler, Degas, and Monet. Fragonard's racy rococo *The Progress of Love* series is installed in a vestibule. You can't say you've seen "all the Vermeers in New York" until you pay homage to the three kept here. Also don't miss Hans Holbein the Younger's pair of incisive portraits of rivals Thomas Cromwell and Sir Thomas More. When humanist scholar and Lord Chancellor Thomas More opposed Henry VIII's divorce, the politically minded Cromwell managed to get More beheaded for treason. Later, Cromwell found himself on Henry VIII's bad side and he, too, lost his head.

The Frick Collection is open Tuesday to Saturday 10am to 6pm, and Sunday 1 to 6pm (closed holidays). Admission is charged, and no children under 10 are admitted (children from ages 10 to 16 must be accompanied by an adult).

Turn right at the corner of Fifth Avenue, passing a beautiful colonnade on the side of the Frick building. Continue two blocks north, and turn right onto 72nd Street, heading toward Madison Avenue. On your left, at no. 9, is the **Lycée Français** (a French primary and secondary school), housed in an elaborate 1894 building of the late French Renaissance style. At the southeast corner of 72nd Street and Madison is:

14. **Polo/Ralph Lauren.** This showcase store, housed in a renovated mansion that dates from 1895, looks for all the world like an English country place, complete with working fireplaces, Persian rugs, antiques, and a grand baronial staircase. The store is closed on Sundays.

Take Madison Avenue up a block to 73rd Street, passing The Sharper Image (no. 900), the catalogue store for the gadget-hound in all of us, and Yumi Katsura (no. 907), a boutique showcasing exquisite wedding gowns for the well-to-do bride. Detour to your left on 73rd Street (past the delectable smells of La Maison du Chocolat) to see:

15. **11 East 73rd St.,** a particularly sumptuous house built in 1903 by McKim, Mead, and White for Joseph Pulitzer, the Hungarian-born publisher of a once-famous but long-vanished newspaper called the *New York World*. Pulitzer rarely lived in this house because of an extreme sensitivity to sound. At one time, it contained a special soundproofed room (mounted on ball bearings, no less) to prevent vibrations. When he died in 1911, Pulitzer bequeathed $2 million to the Columbia Graduate School of Journalism, whose trustees bestow the Pulitzer Prizes, annual awards for outstanding achievement in journalism, literature, drama, and musical composition.

Retrace your steps back to Madison Avenue and turn left. North of 74th Street, you may want to poke your head into the Store Next Door (to the Whitney Museum, that is), with a wonderfully whimsical selection of cards, magnets, T-shirts, clocks, calendars, jewelry, and other creative gifts. On the southeast corner of 75th and Madison, you'll see the:

16. **Whitney Museum of American Art** (☎ 212/ 570-3600), housed in a 1966 architectural masterpiece by Marcel Breuer. The Whitney contains an impressive collection of 20th-century American art, with paintings that reflect trends from naturalism to pop art and abstract expressionism. Roy Lichtenstein, Georgia O'Keeffe, Edward Hopper, and Jasper Johns are just a few of the artists represented here. Hours are Wednesday and Friday to Sunday 11am to 6pm, Thursday 1 to 8pm. Admission is charged.

☕ **Take a Break** In the museum's basement, **Sarabeth's at the Whitney** (☎ 212/570-3670) is much more than your average museum cafeteria—and more expensive, with dishes starting at $13. I had a filling summer vegetable quesadilla, with corn, roasted peppers, cilantro, goat cheese, and a tomato salsa. You might be tempted by the smoked-turkey sandwich with Vermont cheddar cheese. Sarabeth's is also known for its scrumptious desserts (like rice pudding or the chocolate mousse cake with Saboyan) and for its extensive brunch choices (such as pumpkin waffles or granola with fruit, honey, and yogurt).

Though it's housed in the museum, you don't have to pay to reach the cafe; just pick up a free pass at the main ticket desk (you can bypass the museum admissions line).

Leave the museum and continue uptown on Madison Avenue. At 76th Street, you'll pass one of New York's grand old hotels, **the Carlyle,** which has counted two presidents among its famous guests—Harry Truman and John F. Kennedy. The west side of Madison Avenue from 76th to 77th streets is lined with a procession of intriguing contemporary **art galleries**: the Weintraub Gallery at no. 965 (modern sculpture and painting), David Findlay at no. 984 (19th- and 20th-century American and European art), and the best of the lot, the Gagosian Gallery in the penthouse of no. 980 (20th-century artists, including Frank Stella, Richard Serra, Andy Warhol, Mark di Suervo, Chris Burden, and Walter de Maria). Above 77th Street, you'll see fabulously ornate cakes in the window of Sant Ambroeus, an authentic Italian bakery, a good place for a gelato break.

Turn left when you reach 79th Street and return to Fifth Avenue. There's an impressive row of buildings here, everything from French château-style structures to neo-Georgian town houses. When you reach the corner of Fifth Avenue, turn left for a look at:

17. **972 Fifth Ave.,** between 78th and 79th streets. It is now the French Embassy's Cultural Services Office, but it was built in 1906 as a wedding present for Payne Whitney by his doting (and childless) rich uncle, Oliver Payne, a Civil War officer and one of the benefactors who helped to found Cornell's Medical College. This McKim, Mead, and White opus cost $1 million and was the talk of the town in its day. Step inside for a glance at its neoclassical rotunda. The empty pedestal once supported a statue that caused quite a stir in 1995 when a passing art historian pegged it as a long-lost work by Renaissance master Michelangelo. For years having served as a fountain spout, the suddenly famous cupid sculpture has been spirited away until the controversy over its attribution is resolved.

Next door, on the corner of 78th Street, is the classic French-style mansion of tobacco millionaire James B. Duke (as in Duke University). His daughter Doris occupied the house intermittently until 1957, when she donated it to New York University. NYU now operates it as a fine arts institute.

Now turn around and walk north on Fifth Avenue. On your left at 82nd Street is the grand entrance to the:

18. **Metropolitan Museum of Art** (☎ 212/535-7710), one of the world's greatest cultural institutions. The block of 82nd Street that faces the museum's mammoth staircase almost acts as a sort of formal court. The Met's collection is exhaustively enormous—the largest in the western hemisphere—and includes an Egyptian wing that boasts tens of thousands of objects. Its Temple of Dendur, circa 15 B.C. from Lower Nubia, was shipped piece by piece to the Met and painstakingly reconstructed. It would take a lifetime to

see all of the Met's treasures, so it might be best to save it for
another day and merely admire the exterior for now.

Museum hours are Sunday and Tuesday to Thursday
9:30am to 5:15pm, Friday and Saturday 9:30am to 8:45pm.
There's a hefty suggested admission.

Continue uptown to 85th Street. The building at 1040
Fifth Avenue was for many years the:

19. **Home of Jacqueline Kennedy Onassis.** After her
husband's assassination, she moved here so that Caroline
could attend school at nearby Sacred Heart. The former
first lady adored New York, and was often spotted strolling
nearby in her beloved Central Park. After her death from
cancer in 1994, hundreds of mourners gathered outside this
building, many leaving flowers on the sidewalk in her
memory.

Continue uptown to:

20. **86th Street.** The big brick-and-limestone mansion on
the southeast corner of Fifth Avenue and 86th Street was
built in 1914 for William Star Miller. It was to this house
that Mrs. Cornelius Vanderbilt retreated in 1944 when her
famous 640 Fifth Ave. house was sold. No. 640 Fifth Ave.
was located down on 51st Street and was the first of a concentration of family houses that at one time caused Fifth
Avenue in the 1950s to be called "Vanderbilt Alley." By
1944, Mrs. V. was pretty much alone down there, surrounded by ghosts of the Vanderbilt past and lots of noisy
traffic and new office buildings. The exile to 86th Street
appears, at least from the look of this house, to have been
comfortable, anyway.

Two blocks further up Fifth Avenue is the unmistakable:

21. **Guggenheim Museum** (☎ 212/423-3500), between
88th and 89th streets, whose building piques just as much
interest as the collection of 19th- and 20th-century masterpieces it houses. Designed by Frank Lloyd Wright in 1959,
it set off a storm of architectural controversy when it was
built. Nowadays, New Yorkers have grown to think of the
building as a treasured landmark. The structure has a unique
spiral shape; visitors generally take an elevator to the top
floor, then walk down the ramp, viewing the works of art
hung along the curved walls that include many special

exhibitions along with works by Brancusi, Alexander Calder, Marc Chagall, Kadinsky, Paul Klee, Joan Miró, Mondrian, Picasso, and Van Gogh.

The Guggenheim's hours are Sunday to Wednesday 10am to 6pm, Friday and Saturday 10am to 8pm. Admission is charged. Check out the museum store's T-shirts, gifts, prints, and books.

Uptown from the Guggenheim, between 90th and 91st streets, is another major sight, the:

22. **Cooper-Hewitt National Design Museum** (☎ 212/ **860-6872**). Under the auspices of the Smithsonian Institution, it is housed in the former Andrew Carnegie mansion. Built in 1901, this Georgianesque palace originally shared the neighborhood with squatters' shanties and roaming pigs. By the time the squatters were gone and the streets were built up with fine houses, Carnegie was dead. His widow lived in the house until 1949. The museum, with its changing exhibits, is open Tuesday 10am to 9pm, Wednesday to Saturday 10am to 5pm, and Sunday noon to 5pm; a small admission is charged.

Across 91st Street from the main entrance to the Cooper-Hewitt is the:

23. **Convent of the Sacred Heart,** occupying what was once the largest private house ever built in Manhattan. Financier Otto Kahn bought the property from Andrew Carnegie in 1913, and construction of his mansion was completed in 1918. Closely resembling its model, the papal chancellery in Rome, the house is undergoing a major restoration. Other houses on this 91st Street block, notably nos. 7 and 9, are almost as grand.

Take 91st Street east to Madison Avenue and turn right (downtown) if you'd like to end the tour with a pick-me-up.

Winding Down   At the southwest corner of Madison Avenue and 91st Street is **Jackson Hole.** Many New Yorkers argue that Jackson Hole flips the best burgers in the city—and there's no denying that you get a lot for your money. In addition to huge, juicy burgers, Jackson Hole offers omelettes, honey-dipped fried chicken, sandwiches, salads, and great desserts. Forget about your cholesterol count and enjoy. Open daily.

Index

Abrons Arts Center/Harry De Jur Playhouse, 40–41
Adams, Franklin, 118
Adams, George, 125
Adler, Jacob, 102
Agee, James, 72, 76
agnes b., 62
agnes b. homme, 59
Alamo (the Cube), 112–13
Albee, Edward, 78, 89, 91
Albert Apartments, 85
Algonquin Hotel, 118–19
Alice in Wonderland statues, 137
Alice Tully Hall, 152
All-Craft Foundation, 108
All State Cafe, 144–45
Alternative Museum, 54–55
American Ballet Theatre, 152
American Fine Arts Co., 64
American Museum of Natural History, 132, 146–47
American Primitive Gallery, 55
Ansonia Hotel, 144
Anthropologie, 65
Apple Bank for Savings, 145
Apthorp, The, 143
Arsenal, The, 132, 156
Artists Space, 59
Asia Society, 158
Astor Library, 111
Astor Place subway kiosk, 113
Atlas (statue), 122
Atrium, The, 71
Auden, W. H., 101
  home of, 107
Audubon, John James, 147
Avenue of the Americas (Sixth Avenue), 7
Avery Fisher Hall, 151

Balthazar, 55
Bank Street, No. 1, 88
Battery Park, 9
Beat generation, 72–73
Bedford Street, No. 75_, 77
Belvedere Castle, 137
Benchley, Robert, 118
Beresford, The, 147, 148
Berlin Wall, 122
Bethesda Fountain, 135–36
Bialystoker Synagogue, 40
Bleecker, Anthony, 70
Bleecker Street, 70
Bloody Angle, 29
Boathouse Café, 136
Boone, Mary, Gallery, 126
Bowery Gallery, 62–63
Bowling Green Park, 11
Broadway, 5, 6
"Broken Kilometer, The," 65
Brooke Alexander Projects, 63
Bull, in front of 25 Broadway, 12
Burns, Robert, statue of, 135

Café des Artistes, 150
Café Figaro, 72
Café Pierre, 129
Café St. Bart's, 124
Caffè Cino, 76–77
Canal Street, 24, 25
Carlyle Hotel, 161
Carnegie, Andrew, 164
Carousel, The (Central Park), 134
Cast-Iron Building (Broadway & 11th Street), 95–96
Cavin-Morris, 52
Central Park, 128–39
Central Park West, 7, 146-148

Central Park Wildlife Conservation Center (Central Park Zoo), 129, 132, 156
Central Synagogue, 125
Chatham Club, 29
Chatham Square, 26
Chelsea, 5
Cherry Lane Theatre, 78
Chess and Checkers House, 133
Chinatown, 4, 22–36
Chinatown Fair, 30
Chinatown History Museum, 33
Chinese Consolidated Benevolent Association (CCBA), 27, 29, 32
Chinese Exclusion Act (1882), 24
Chinese Merchants Association (On Leong), 32
Chinese New Year, 30
Chinese School, 32
Christadora House, 107
Christopher Street, Waverly Place &, 81
Chrysler Building, 117–18
Chumley's, 78
Church of Sea and Land, 35
Church of the Transfiguration, 31
Circle in the Square Theater, 71
Citarella, 143
C. i. t. e., 63
Citicorp Center, 124
City Hall, 19–20
City Hall Park, 19
Cleopatra's Needle (Obelisk), 138

Collegiate School, 143
Colonnade Row, 112
Columbia Graduate School of
    Journalism, 160
Columbus, Christopher,
    statue of, 135
Columbus Avenue, 145
Columbus Park, 33–34
Comme des Garçons, 63
Commerce mural (Jennewein),
    19
Commerce Street, No. 11, 77
Confucius, statue of, 27
Confucius Plaza, 26
Conservatory Garden, 139
Conservatory Water, 137
Convent of the Sacred Heart,
    164
Cooper, Peter
    statue of, 110–11
Cooper-Hewitt National
    Design Museum, 164
Cooper Square, 110
Cooper Union Foundation
    Building, 110, 111
Cornelia Street, No. 33, 76
C. R. G. Gallery, 59
Cunard Building, 12
Cupping Room Cafe, 64
Customs House, U. S., 9, 11

Dairy, The (Central Park),
    133–34
Dakota, The, 148
Danspace, 101
David Sarnoff Building
    (Educational Alliance),
    41–42
Dean and Deluca, 50, 52, 85
Delacorte Clock, 133
Delacorte Theater, 137
Delancey Street, 46
Delano and Aldrich, 156
DIA Center for the Arts, 62
Dial (magazine), 87
Diamond District, 119
Dim sum, 27, 28
Din Lay Co., 30–31
Doyers Street, 28, 29
Drawing Center, The, 64

East 11th Street, 85
East 64th Street, No. 3,
    156–57
East 66th Street, No. 3, 157
East 68th Street, No. 58, 157
East 70th Street, 158
East 73rd Street, No. 11, 160
East 86th Street, 163
East Broadway Mall, 35–36
Eastern States Buddhist
    Temple of America, 32
East Village, 4, 5, 92–113
Educational Alliance (the
    David Sarnoff Building),
    41–42
Edward Mooney House, 26
Eighth Avenue, 7

Eileen's Special Cheesecake,
    56
Eldridge Street Project, 43
Eldridge Street Synagogue,
    43–44
Electric Circus, 108–9
Elga Wimmer, 52
Ellen's Café and Bake Shop,
    20
Enchanted Forest, The, 57
Essex Street Pickles, 44

Fairway, 143
Fanelli's Cafe, 60
Fantino Restaurant, 129
F. A. O. Schwarz, 126
Federal Hall National
    Memorial, 13–14
Ferrucci's Gourmet Market,
    104
Fifth Avenue, 7, 156, 162
Financial District, 2
Financial District and Lower
    Manhattan, 8–21
First Chinese Presbyterian
    Church, 35
First Shearith Israel
    Graveyard, 34
Fish market, Chinatown, 25
Forbes Magazine Building, 86
Forward, The (newspaper),
    42–43
Forward Building, 42–43
Fraunces Tavern, 12–13
Fraunces Tavern Museum, 12
French, Daniel Chester, 9
French Embassy's Cultural
    Services Office, 162
Frick Collection, 159–60
Fuller Building, 125

Gagosian Gallery, 62, 161–62
Gallery Guide, The, 53
Gay Street, 81
GE Building, 120–21
Gem Spa, 108
General Slocum (ferry), 106
George Adams, 125
Golden Pacific National
    Bank, 25
Golden Unicorn, 27–28
Gotham Book Mart, 119–20
Gourmet Garage, 58
Grace Church, 96–98
Grace Memorial House, 98
Grand Army Plaza, 129, 154
Grand Central Terminal,
    116–17
Grand Street, Nos. 91-93, 59
Grant, Cary, 77
Grant, Ulysses S., home of,
    157
Great Lawn, Central Park,
    138
Greeley, Horace, 82
    statue of, 19
Greenberg, Howard, Gallery,
    63

Greene Street, 58
Greenwich Avenue, 88, 89
Greenwich Village (West
    Village), 4, 5
    literary tour, 67–91
Grove Street, 79, 80
Guggenheim Bandshell, 152
Guggenheim Museum, 127,
    163–64
Guggenheim Museum SoHo,
    54
Gunther Building, 59
Guss Pickle Products, 44

Haas, Richard, Mural, 60
Hale, Nathan, statue of, 19
Halleck, Fitz-Greene, 82
    statue of, 135
Hallett Nature Sanctuary,
    133
Hall of Records, The
    (Surrogate's Court), 20–21
H & H Bagels, 143
*Hans Christian Andersen
    Memorial Statue*, 137
Hans Holbein the Younger,
    159–60
Harriet Love, 62
Harry De Jur Playhouse,
    40–41
Harvard Club, 118
Haughwout Building, 56
Hebrew Actors Union, 109
Hebrew Immigrant Aid
    Society, 111–12
Hebrew Religious Articles, 44
Helmsley Building, 123
Henry Street Settlement, 40,
    41
Herter Brothers, 43
Hip Sing tong, 29
Hirschl and Adler, 159
HMV, 144
Holly Solomon Gallery, 60
Holmes, John Clellon, 72
Hotel Albert, 85
Hotel des Artistes, 150
Howard Greenberg Gallery,
    63
Hunter College, 158

Indian Hunter (statue), 135
International Center of
    Photography, 119

Jackson Hole, 164
Jack Tilton Gallery, 59
James Joyce Society, 120
Jazz Vespers, 124
Jefferson Market Library, 90
Jekyll and Hyde, 60
Jewish Lower East Side,
    37–47
Jewish Rialto, 102
Joseph Papp Public Theater,
    111–12
Julliard School, 152
Justice (statue), 19

Kalikow Building, 17–18
Kam Man Food Inc., 33
Kate's Paperie, 53
Katz's Delicatessen, 47
Kimlau War Memorial, 34
Kind, Phyllis, Gallery, 61
King Cole Bar and Lounge, 127
"King of Greene Street," 59
Knickerbocker Bar and Grill, 85
Knickerbocker Club, 156
Knoedler and Company, 159
Kossar's Bialys, 44

Labor mural (Jennewein), 19
Ladies' Mile, 95, 96, 98
Lafayette Street, 55–56, 112
LaGuardia, Fiorello, 117
Le Cirque 2000, 123
Leo Castelli, 66
Lexington Avenue, 7
Liberal Club, 75, 83
Liberator (magazine), 87
Liberty Plaza, 15
Lincoln Center, 140, 151–52
Little Italy, 4
Living Theatre, 78
Loeb Boathouse, 136
Louis K. Meisel Gallery, 65
Lower East Side, 4
    Jewish, 37–47
Lower East Side Tenement Museum, 45–46
Lower Manhattan. *See* Financial District and Lower Manhattan
Lycée Français, 160

MacDougal Street, 73–75
McKee Gallery, 126
McKim, Mead, and White, 21, 118, 123, 157, 160, 162
McSorley's Old Ale House and Grill, 109–10
Madison Avenue, 7
Majestic Apartments, 149
Mall, The (Central Park), 135
Manhattan Bridge, 26
Marie's Crisis Cafe, 80
Mariner's Temple, 35
Marlborough Gallery, 126
Marques, Rachel Rodriguez, 34
Marriott Hotel, 16
Mary Boone Gallery, 126
Masses, The (magazine), 88
Meisel, Louis K., Gallery, 65
Memorial Arch, 83
Mercedes-Benz showroom, 125
Mercer Street, No. 105, 57
Metropolitan Museum of Art, 162–63
Metropolitan Museum of Art Shop, 62

Metropolitan Opera House, 151–52
Midtown, 114–27
Millay, Edna St. Vincent, 74, 77, 78, 82, 88, 118
Minetta Brook, 73, 82
Minetta Tavern, 73
Ming Fay Book Store, 32
Mitzi Newhouse Theater, 152
Miu Miu, 60
Moss, 61
Mott Street, 30
Mulberry Bend, 34
Mulberry Street, 4, 33
Municipal Building, 21
Museum for African Art, The, 54
Museum of American Folk Art annex and gift shop, 151
Museum of Modern Art (MoMA)
    bookshop, 122

Nancy Hoffman, 65
Nancy's Wines for Food, 145–46
National Museum of the American Indian, Smithsonian's, 9, 11
Natural History, American Museum of, 132, 146–47
New Lung Fong Bakery, 31
New Museum of Contemporary Art, The, 54
New School for Social Research, 86
New York City Ballet, 151
New York City Opera, 151
New York County Courthouse (Tweed Courthouse), 20
New Yorker, The, 53, 118–19
New York Historical Society, 147–48
New York magazine, 53
New York Palace Hotel, 123
New York Public Library, 117, 152
New York Shakespeare Festival, 112
New York Stock Exchange, 13
New York Times, 53
Nice Restaurant, 27
Nieuw Amsterdam, 9
Ninth Avenue, 7
Ninth Circle, 89
Noonday Concert series, 15, 18
Novy Mir (periodical), 107

O. K. Harris, 65
Obelisk (Cleopatra's Needle), 138
Onassis, Jacqueline Kennedy, 116
    home of, 163

On Leong (Chinese Merchants Association), 32
Orchard Street, 38, 46–47
Ottendorfer Library, 102–3
Oyster Bar, 116–17

Pace Master Prints and Drawings, 125
Pace Primitive Art, 125
Pace Prints, 126
Pace-Wildenstein Gallery, 61, 125
Pace-Wildenstein-MacGill, 125
Park Avenue, 7, 158–59
Patchin Place, 90
Peale, Rembrandt, 20
Pearl Paint, 58
Pearl Theatre Company, 108
Pell Street, 29
Phyllis Kind Gallery, 61
Pierre, The, 154, 156
Plaza Hotel, 127, 129
Poetry Project, 101
Polo/Ralph Lauren, 160
Pond, The (Central Park), 133
Pop Shop, 56
Prometheus (Manship), 120
Provincetown Playhouse, 74–75
Public Theater, Joseph Papp, 111–12
Pulitzer Prizes, 160

"Queen of Greene Street," 58
Quintero, Jose, 71
Quong Yuen Shing & Company, 30

Radio City Music Hall, 121
Ramble, the, 137
Ratner's Dairy Restaurant, 38, 40
RCA Building, 120
Renwick Triangle, 100
Republic Bank for Savings, 25–26
Reservoir, Central Park, 139
Ricco/Maresca Gallery, 62
Richard Haas Mural, 60
Robert Miller, 125
Rockefeller Center, 120–21
Rockefeller Plaza, No. 30, 120–21
Roland Feldman Fine Arts, 58
Roosevelt, Theodore, 123
    statue of, 147
Round Table, 118
Royalton Hotel, 119
Russian-Turkish Baths, 104–5
Russo's Mozzarella and Pasta Corp., 104

St. Bartholomew's church, 124
St. Denis Hotel, 96

Saint-Gaudens, Augustus, 111, 154
St. George's Ukrainian Catholic Church, 110
Saint Mark's-in-the-Bowery, 99, 100–101
St. Marks Place, 108
St. Nicholas Hotel, 57
St. Patrick's Cathedral, 122
St. Paul's Chapel, 18
St. Peter's Lutheran Church, 124
St. Regis Hotel, 127
Saks Fifth Avenue, 120
Salmagundi Club, 86
Saloon, The, 152
San Remo (Carpo's Cafe), 72–73
San Remo, The (apartment building), 148
Sant Ambroeus, 162
Sarabeth's at the Whitney, 161
Schwarz, F. A. O., 126
Sean Kelly, 58
Second Avenue Deli, 101
Segal, George, 81
Sert, José Maria, 121
Shakespeare, William, statue of, 135
Shakespeare Garden, 138
Shakespeare in the Park series, 137
Sharper Image, The, 160
Sheep Meadow, 135
Sheridan Square Park, 81
Sherman, William Tecumseh, statue of, 154
Singer Building, 53
Sinotique, 31
Sixth Avenue (Avenue of the Americas), 7
and West 4th Street, 76
Smart Set (magazine), 118
Smithsonian's National Museum of the American Indian, 9, 11
SoHo, 2, 4, 48–66
SoHo Grand Hotel, 66
Solomon, Holly, Gallery, 60
Sonnabend Gallery, 66
Sons of Israel Kalwarie Synagogue, 36
Spring Street, No. 101, 57
Stamp Act Congress, 14
Stonewall, The (Stonewall Inn), 80–81
Store Next Door, 161
Strand Bookstore, 93, 95
Strawberry Fields, 149
Stuyvesant-Fish House, 98, 100

Stuyvesant Polyclinic Hospital, 102, 103
Stuyvesant Street, 98, 100
Surma, 110
Surrogate's Court (The Hall of Records), 20–21
Synagogue of the Congregation Shearith Israel, 150

Tavern on the Green, 134
Taylor, Thomas House, 97
Tea and Sympathy, 87–88
Temperance Fountain, 106
Tenth Avenue, 7
Tenth Street Baths, 104–5
Theater for the New City (TNC), 104
Theatre 80 St. Marks, 108
Tiffany & Co., 126
Tilton, Jack, Gallery, 59
Todd Oldham Store, 62
Tompkins Square Park, 106–7
Tongs, 29
Transfiguration, Church of the, 31
Traveller's Bookstore, 122
Trinity Church, 14
Tweed Courthouse (New York County Courthouse), 20
Twenty-one Club, 121

Ukrainian Museum, 103
Ukrainian National Home, 101–2
Ukrainian Restaurant, 101
Union Club, 158
Untermeyer Fountain, 139
Upper East Side, 5, 153–64
Upper West Side, 5, 140–52
Urban Center, 123
U. S. Customs House, 9, 11

Vanity Fair, 118
Vegetable sellers, Chinatown, 25
Veniero's Pasticceria, 103–4
Vesuvio Bakery, 65–66
Village Voice, The, 53, 111
Villard Houses, 123
Vivian Beaumont Theater, 152

Waldorf-Astoria, 123–24
Wall Street, 9, 14
Wanamaker Department Store Annex, 98
Ward, J. Q. A., 14, 19, 135
Warren and Wetmore, 156

Washington, George, 18
statue of, 14
Washington Mews, 84
Washington Place, 82
Washington Square (James), 83
Washington Square Book Shop, 75
Washington Square North (Waverly Place), 83–84
Washington Square Park, 70, 82–83
Waterfall
53rd Street between Fifth and Madison Avenues, 122
in 666 Fifth Avenue building, 122
Waverly Place, 81, 82
Weinfeld's Skull Cap Mfg., 44
Weintraub Gallery, 161
West 3rd Street, No. 85, 74
West 10th Street, 89, 91
West 13th Street, 87
West 52nd Street, 121–22
West 75th Street, No. 150, 146
West 84th Street, No. 215, 141
West End Collegiate Church and School, 143
West Village. *See* Greenwich Village
Whitney Museum of American Art, 161
Windows on the World, 16–17
Winter Garden, 17
Wisteria Pergola, 139
Wollman Rink, 133
Wonderful Town, 81
Woolworth Building, 18–19
World Financial Center, 17
World Trade Center (WTC), 16–17
Wright, Frank Lloyd, 125, 127, 163
Writers' Emergency Fund, 120
Wylie, Elinor, 118

Yacht Club, 118
Yohji Yamamoto, 58
York and Sawyer, 145
Yumi Katsura, 160

Zabar's, 141, 143
Zona, 60
Zoo, Central Park (Central Park Wildlife Conservation Center), 129, 132, 156
Zoo Café, 129